The Trickster's Hat

A Mischievous Apprenticeship in Creativity

Nick Bantock

A PERIGEE BOOK

A PERIGEE BOOK
Published by the Penguin Group
Penguin Group (USA) LLC
375 Hudson Street, New York, New York 10014

USA | Canada | UK | Ireland | Australia | New Zealand | India | South Africa | China

penguin.com

A Penguin Random House Company

THE TRICKSTER'S HAT
Copyright © 2014 by Nick Bantock

ISBN: 978-0-399-16502-3

An application to catalog this book has been submitted to the Library of Congress.

First edition: January 2014

PRINTED IN THE UNITED STATES OF AMERICA
10 9 8 7 6 5 4 3 2 1

Nick Bantock: Words, images, and design
Brian (Joost) Foot: Design, typography, and digital production
Joyce Bantock: Studio assistant, and sanity anchor
David Borrowman: Fine art photography

Found curdled @ Post Office

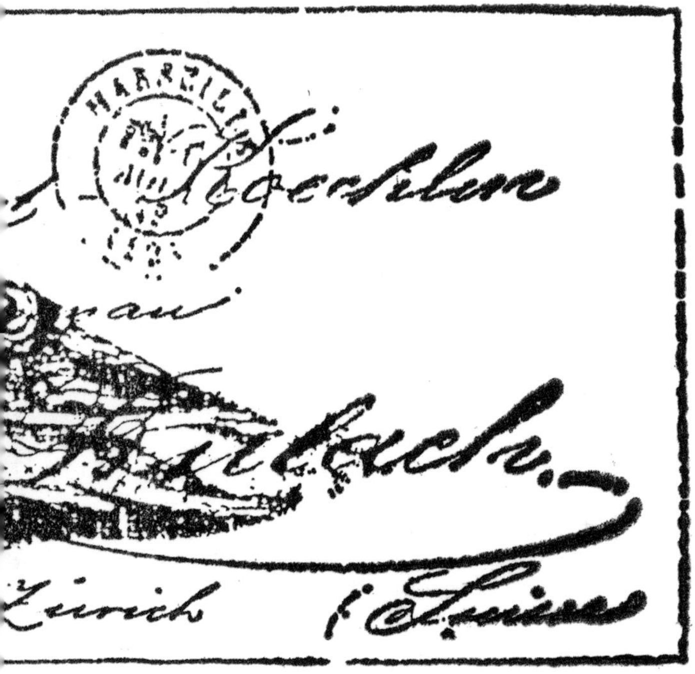
Zürich

For the wide-eyed wonderers

CONTENTS

If you want a shortcut 1

The Exercises

1   Climbing in Through a Small Window 16
2   Loosening the Brain 18
3   Stamp Collage 20
4   Pictorial Autobiography 22
5   Directed Collage 26
6   Finishing Lines 32
7   Building a Country 36
8   Composition 42
9   Transposing Nouns 46
10 Portrait of the Artist as a Young Man 50
11 Traveling with Archetypes 52
12 Limerick 60
13 First Kiss 62
14 A Rant 64
15 Inventing Words 70
16 Dice Game 72
17 Porky Pies or Passionate Lies 76
18 Board Game 80
19 The Unusual Suspects 82
20 Ice and Fire 86
21 Four-Square Collage 88
22 Lost in the Forest 92
23 Poetry of Silence 96
24 Altered Models 100

25	Face Collage	104
26	Chiaroscuro	106
27	Form and Content	110
28	Mundane vs. Romantic	112
29	Graphic Quotes	116
30	A Marriage of Opposites	120
31	Learning from Others	124
32	Magical Object	128
33	The Unexpected	130
34	Envelope	132
35	Drawing Empty	134
36	Sage	140
37	Dreams	144
38	Top Fives	150
39	Blue	152
40	Expanding the Jabberwocky	154
41	Climbing the Steps	158
42	Big Pastel	164
43	Reverse Time Capsules	166
44	Childmind	168
45	Lopsided Lighthouse	172
46	Painting Without Brushes	174
47	Risk and Happy Accidents	178
48	Delivered by Accident in Twilight	180
49	Seduction Optional	184
	And Then...	188
	Index of the Familiars	192

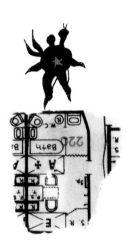

A WARNING

If you want a shortcut to originality... this isn't the book for you.

On the other hand, if you're willing to be led hither and thither down unlikely paths by a fellow of dubious reputation, if you're prepared to keep a sense of humor and not be fazed when he plucks the unexpected out of a mischief-stuffed hat, if you're ready to zigzag, detour, and wander in search of a better understanding of your artistic core, then please feel free to slip-slide further into these pages.

"QUARTER-INCH" MAP
FOURTH EDITION

✖ WHERE TO START

It's dusk. A stranger is driving around the countryside utterly lost. Eventually he comes to a tiny hamlet. The place is deserted apart from a little man sitting on a rustic fence. The stranger winds his window down and asks for directions to Fortunes Hall. The little man removes his peculiar, battered hat, places it upside down between his knees, scratches his head, and without looking up begins.

"It's like this," he says. "You take the first right, the third left, the second right, pass over the humpback bridge, then you carry on till you reach the Goat's Arms. A mile after that you'll see..." and so he continues for a full two minutes.

Finally he completes the impossibly convoluted stream of directions, replaces his hat, fixes the stranger with a piercing gaze, and declares, "But if I were you, I wouldn't start from here."

Our friend the stranger has a problem. If you were he, what would you do next? You cannot retrace your steps. There is no one else to ask. Are you obliged to keep driving in the hope that you will stumble on your destination before the night descends?

A troublesome conundrum – or maybe not. If you are less specific about your destination, then maybe you aren't lost at all.

WHO IS THE TRICKSTER, AND WHAT ELSE DOES HE HAVE IN HIS HAT?

Of all the reasons for being an artist, there is one that outweighs all others: Art offers a path to our souls.

But this path isn't direct. There are no shortcuts. The road is confusing, and seemingly getting lost along the way is inevitable.

However, perhaps that is the point. After all, if it were simply a matter of going from A to B as the crow flies, how much would we learn along the way? In order to gather wisdom, we are obliged to stumblebum, our search careening us against the periphery of our comfort and comprehension.

By nature these wanderings aren't easy. We have been told so many times that if we want something badly enough and focus hard enough, we can have it. But that concept falls prey to the notion that we can conceive what we need, that we know the best way to go, that there *is* a best way to go. We can't get far enough back from the road to see the topography: our perception of where we might be going will thankfully always be wrong.

And that's where the Trickster comes in. Having a wise-joker as our journey's companion—someone whose very nature embodies misdirection—is an enormous asset, and we need all the help we can get. So, for the duration of this book, the Trickster—who comes ready furnished with a map and an exercise hat—will be joining us. He has much to give, but remember: he has no qualms about tripping us awake if our boots get too filled with ego.

A PIGMENT OF THE IMAGINATION

Have you ever tried setting your mind to an intentionally impossible task? For example, trying to grasp infinity or eternity, imagining colors that aren't on the spectrum, or attempting to rhyme purple, silver, and orange?

The exercise is not intended to be one of frustration but of widening expectation and stretching the imagination so that it's more willing to encompass the less obvious.

Among other things, the Trickster (and his family of Familiars, see page 192) teaches us how to go outside our standard way of observing things. He helps us expand our peripheral vision, to see beyond the obvious path.

As I understand it, civilization needs something approaching a shared view of reality in order to function. But that norm is inevitably narrow and blinkered. None of us really see, hear, and experience exactly the same thing as our neighbors; we merely agree on a colluded approximation, hoping that if we cling together we won't get too disoriented.

But our peripheral vision functions outside the agreed-upon norm and observes not just parts of but all of our sensory experiences. By bringing this "outside stuff" into focus, we gain inspiration.

Reality may pretend to exist—but it's got no imagination.

When people (not only artists) expand their vision, they intentionally widen themselves to a different or original version of things.

Close your eyes. Look as far as you can to the left and the right. See if you can see a purple-black universe where great archaic wooden machines with clanking wheels churn out spiraling motes of gold dust.

LETTING THE CAT OUT...

If we are to see beyond the periphery, we must first learn how to let go of self-seriousness and relearn the art of play. The Trickster's job is to teach you how to teach yourself, and as strange as his meandering directions may sometimes seem, he has your best interests at heart. The projects and exercises that make up the bulk of these pages are highly varied, but the substance behind them remains the same. If you can learn how to tap into your true motivations and passions, then your creative drive will automatically follow. But to find those driving forces you'll need to loosen the reins and take on the mantle of mischief.

From my perspective there are two main barriers that limit artistic power, whatever your medium of expression happens to be: developing technical skill and overcoming the blocks that restrict our creative potential. While this book is highly respectful of the former, its focus is on the latter.

If we trust the Trickster and his process of expanding imagination beyond the periphery, then the rewards are a never-ending enthusiasm for life, the universe, and everything!

KEEPING ONE FOOT ON THE SHORE

In order to help unearth the roots of creativity, the exercises here are designed to prod and poke the psyche, which means you might sometimes find yourself a bit stirred up without really knowing why. But worry not—this isn't therapy. Therapy attempts to break down obstruction and assist through a cathartic release. I'm more interested in teaching ways to set free a creative energy that will flow onto the paper without judgment and analytical observation of its origin. Each of us has within us a mother lode of creative fuel that, when accessed, can ignite our artistic process in a way that will keep us going for years.

If, while you are doing one of the exercises, a strong emotion starts to rise, try to stay focused on the work in front of you. An old friend of mine calls it "keeping one foot on the shore." You take notice that you feel a shift, but you don't allow yourself to go flying off on a cathartic surfboard. If you say, "Isn't that interesting, now I'm mad at my old schoolteacher for making fun of me in front of the class," then continue writing or painting so that your recollection becomes a catalyst for the art that passes onto the page.

It's amazing how often I've seen this kind of noncritical self-observation assist people in growing meaning and significance in their works.

And lo, the emotion that hasn't killed you makes you a better artist!

WHY COLLAGE

The primary medium we'll use throughout this workshop is collage. Not in the small sense of the word but *collage* in its broadest form, which includes everything from art and writing to humorous ranting and steampunking Barbie dolls. Unlike many art forms, collage is both highly flexible and forgiving. It's also fast changing and nonlinear, which tends to promote a sense of euphoric freedom from the predictable.

Whether you have been an artist all your life or you've only just started to explore, the playing field will be level; the exercises I've set out are accessible and far from exclusive. So, please, don't be intimidated. Just treat each task as a chance to be playful. The more you throw yourself into each activity, the more you will get back from it.

ARTFULLY DODGING THE ROADBLOCKS

Before you begin the exercises in earnest, ask yourself what you hope to get from participation. Obviously you haven't read the rest of the book yet, but my guess is you already have a rough idea of what you hope to gain. What is that? What do you want to know? What part of yourself do you want to liberate? Now ask yourself what's going to stop you. How do you invariably block yourself from getting what you most need? We all find ways to undermine ourselves. And, if you know those ways in which you obstruct yourself, maybe you can avoid the pattern and allow what follows to feed your most pressing needs.

PRACTICAL STUFF

You'll notice that there are no computers involved in any of these tasks. That's not because I'm a Luddite, but because I want you to experience the two-way relationship that can grow between your hands and the materials you're using—a symbiosis that can generate a very specific kind of learning, one that calls for a greater sense of risk. A computer gives you the option of hitting a key and going back a previous layer, but you can't do that with paint and paper. You have to keep moving forward, and the momentum will help you understand a very different level of emotional commitment.

When we get to each exercise, I'll tell you up front what materials you'll need. Sometimes it will be as simple as a pencil and a scrap of paper, and sometimes it will be more specific materials. I've purposely tried to design things so that the majority of these exercises can be completed with the list of basic materials. I'm also going to include the approximate time each exercise will take. If you give yourself that time (distraction free) and you have the right equipment in front of you, you'll find it so much easier than if you allow any distractions or have to go scrabbling off to find the right brush or a glue stick that isn't rock hard.

Although the majority of the exercises that follow involve art and writing, this book is for anyone who wants to widen their perspective and is prepared to chance the Trickster's crooked path.

Finally, I encourage you to do the exercises in order, but it's not the end of the world if you hop around a bit. Find your own pace. The only thing I ask is that you give yourself permission to have fun and enjoy the fireworks of your imagination.

E X R

E C

I S S

>

E

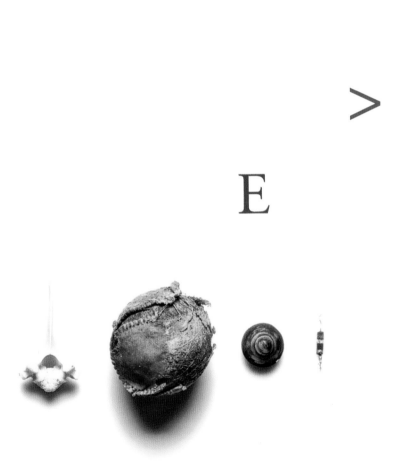

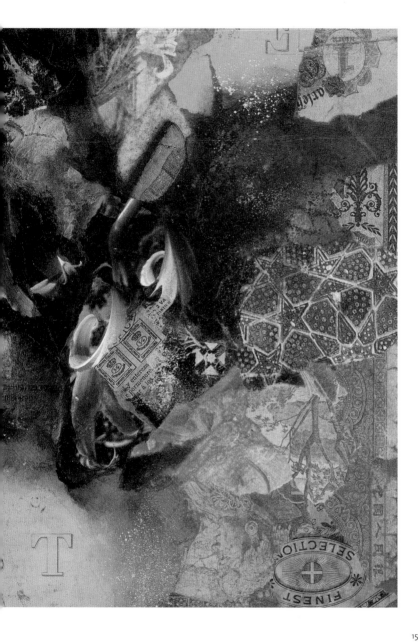

1

Climbing in Through a Small Window

Getting started can be the hardest part of the working day. I always make sure that when I go into the studio I do something that I feel like doing and not something I should or ought to do. Even if it's only for the first twenty minutes, it's important to be obligation free.

Whether you want to start something fresh or pick up where you left off the previous day, the anxiety around beginning or screwing up what you've already done will likely turn you into a procrastinator. But if, before you take on anything meaty, you just doodle or splash paint onto a bit of paper or scrap of board, you can cut through some of the self-doubts and resentments about having dragged yourself away from the comfy chair.

In this first exercise, we're going to climb into the arena, unannounced, and through a very small window.

Materials: paper and mechanical pencil or fine-tipped pen
Time: 10 minutes
Size: 2" × 2"

INSTRUCTIONS

Draw a 2" x 2" square. Inside the square, draw as many animals as you can in five minutes. (It's up to you how you interpret that.)

Now draw a second 2" x 2" square, but leave one of the four sides open. Then draw as many animals as you can escaping out of the square. Again, you have five minutes.

HINT

This is not about drawing skills; it's not a test. It's about doing something relatively lighthearted that gets you moving. But mostly it's to remind yourself that you need to enjoy what you're doing.

Loosening the Brain

If you still feel mentally tight or for any other reason not ready to start on anything challenging, don't try to force yourself. Better to loosen up first, like athletes stretching out their muscles. Try this as an unwinder.

Materials: fat black pencil (I recommend a 3B or softer) and 2 sheets of paper (newsprint will work)
Time: 2 or 3 minutes
Size: not less than 12" x 12"

INSTRUCTIONS

Using your left hand if you are right-handed, or vice versa, quickly draw a circle, a triangle, a square, and a pentagon, all on the same sheet of paper. Keep drawing geometric shapes, not worrying about their accurateness. Continue for about a minute, filling the page. Then get a new sheet of paper and switch to your other hand. This time keep your arm stretched away from your body and start scribbling and making short slashed marks. What it looks like doesn't matter; what counts is the devil-may-care attitude.

HINT

Concentrate on the feel of the pencil in your hand rather than the shapes you are drawing. Make sure you breathe right into the pit of your belly as you doodle away.

Three minutes in total should be ample time to loosen your brain and get you ready to focus on whatever work is calling.

Stamp Collage

Stamps can be very addictive. Little capsules of history, geography, and art, they suck you into their world. Once you enter, your chances of escape from their gravity are slim. I got hooked over 30 years ago, and they still intrigue me as intensely as they did the day I first walked into the old Corn Exchange stamp shop in Bristol. I collected seriously for years but kicked the habit when I started inventing my own countries and designing their stamps!

Most cities have a stamp store, and they will be more than willing to sell you a bag of cheap stamps for collaging. Alternatively, have a poke around on eBay, and you'll be able to find some for very little there. The vast majority of stamps are worth less than a cent apiece, so picking up a boxful of them for collaging is going to cost you little more than pocket change.

While you probably wouldn't want to attempt a large collage using only stamps, for small or miniature collages they are perfect. Packed with color and content and on a suitable weight of paper, you can cut and paste them with abandon.

Materials: scrap of white paper, pencil, old stamps, and glue stick
Time: 20 minutes
Size: 3" × 1.5"

INSTRUCTIONS

Draw a 3" × 1.5" rectangle on the paper. Using stamps as your collage material, construct a landscape in your rectangle. For this exercise, the stamps must be torn. No cutting, except for creating straight edges to use against the sides of your frame line. When tearing paper, have the piece you want to use in your dominant hand and rip toward you— that way you'll avoid an unwanted white edge.

Also, don't use any figurative elements from the stamps—a tree shouldn't be used as a tree.

HINT

Get rid of the perforations and white border from around the stamps or they'll make your collage look like crazy paving. Treat the little torn sections of stamp as if they are part of a mosaic, building your landscape piece by piece.

Pictorial Autobiography

An editor once told me that the majority of first novels should be ditched as soon as they are completed because they will inevitably be a thinly disguised justification of one's own existence – "I'm right and you were all wrong!"

As harsh as that is, there are probably a few grains of truth there. We all need to tell our life story once, to give our version of who and why we are, if only to feel that we have been seen and heard. But rather than spending a year or two battling with 350 pages of text, you might want to try the following pictorial autobiography. It's a way to get your version of events out of your system in under a couple of hours.

Materials: old black-and-white prints, cartoons, and engravings; posterboard or heavyweight paper; scissors; and matte medium and brush
Time: 90 minutes
Size: 3 squares, each 6" × 6"
◗ Matte medium or gel is the best material for adhering paper for collage. Using a brush, apply the medium to the ground (paper, board, or panel), then to the back of the paper you are collaging; stick the paper down and put a further thin coat of medium over the top.

INSTRUCTIONS

The idea here is to create three black-and-white collages in a cartoon-like triptych. The first square should represent your childhood, the second your teens and youth, and the third your adulthood. I'm suggesting you restrict your palette to black and white for two reasons: first, because it's hard enough to tell your life story in three pictures without having to deal with the complexities of color balancing; and second, because black and white tends to give history authenticity (personal or otherwise).

Of course, it's an insane task if you try to include all of the main events in your life. Therefore, you'll need to find elements or symbols that represent the general tone of who you were and the events that surrounded you. It's important not to use your real family photos or ephemera; that's too likely to enslave you in a dry history.

Because you are working with found material, you will have to be flexible and inventive. Don't obsess on finding a specific image. Personally, I find it easier to avoid premeditation, working the opposite way around, looking for images that point less directly to elements of my past. Sometimes these can be quite obscure, yet they often have a way of being more poignant than any literal illustration of triumphs and disasters.

HINT

I once picked up six old bound copies of *Punch* yearbooks. *Punch* was a humorous magazine full of elegantly drawn cartoons and line engravings, and it proved perfect for this exercise. Try your local secondhand bookstore to see what they have in the way of beaten-up old illustrated magazines or annuals.

In case you are wondering, as a general rule in the United States, there are fairly minimal copyright restrictions on printed materials more than seventy years old.

ferent

D,

Priče 1o. 6.

VG.

Son.

Directed Collage

In my experience, this next exercise can have a polarizing effect, and my guess is you'll find it to be liberating or constricting. Either way, it will offer you a useful method of getting your collage started. Decision making in art, as anywhere else, can be exhausting, so being directed step by step can take away some of the pressure. However, if you hate being told what to do, this list is likely to make you want to regress into a state of "I won't, I won't!" That's fine—take note that that's your knee-jerk reaction and then do it anyway.

I'm going to give you a bunch of simple instructions. Follow each one in order, and don't think too hard about what you are doing; in fact, try not to think at all—just do it. Take no more than a couple of minutes for each task. Working fast is key. Sometimes the instructions will be open ended and you'll have choices, but don't let that distract you. First thoughts are best. For example, if I say, "Add a blue triangle," you could paint it, draw it, or cut it out of paper and adhere it. There's no wrong solution; whatever medium you choose is okay. At this early stage, composition doesn't come into it.

If you can do this exercise with a friend, all the better. They can be in the same room with you, or you can even pair up with a friend in a different location. You'll see why I suggest this when we get to the second and third parts of the collage.

Materials: acrylic paints, paintbrush, white(ish) posterboard,
colored pencils or crayons, chalk pastels, varied old magazines,
scissors, tissue paper, and matte medium and brush
Time: 2 hours minimum
Size: anywhere between 12"x 10" and 16"x 13"

INSTRUCTIONS

▸ Select any tube of paint. Using a thin mixed solution of that color,
  quickly cover half your board with a largish paintbrush.
  (Keep in mind there are many different ways of covering half.)

▸ Take a colored pencil (or crayon) and scribble rapidly on the
  remaining white half of the board.

▸ Add a red triangle.

▸ Add a number (hand done or torn from a magazine or newspaper).

▸ Add a bigger number, this time making it touch up against the edge
  of your board.

▸ Pick a chalk pastel, draw on half of the remaining white area,
  and rub it in with your fingers.

▸ Tear out a figure from a magazine (could be human or animal)
  and adhere it to your picture.

▸ Select another tube of paint. Mix that color with a little black and
  a little white. Use the mixed color to paint out the remaining area
  of white on your picture.

I don't want you to get too precise about any of these instructions. We are really just building the ground in order to create some layers.

- Squeeze a small amount of blue paint onto the heel of your hand, then without thinking about placement, bang your hand down onto your picture three times.
- Tear a piece of tissue paper and paste it down onto your piece with matte medium, then paint over the top of the tissue with more matte medium. (When it dries, not only will it be well stuck, but it will be sealed in, so that you will be able to continue to work on top of it.)
- Quickly scan the magazines looking for a map or a diagram, rip a corner section out, and put it in one corner of your picture.
- Go back to the magazines and look for something "unexpected." Put it in the opposite corner of the map/diagram.

By now the picture may be feeling messy. Messy is okay. We are just developing the necessary layers.

- Find a largish letter (alphabet, not mail!), cut it in half, and add it to your picture so that the two cut sections are butted against different edges.
- STOP. Look at what you've done so far. Push any judgment from your mind. Just absorb what's there without taking critical responsibility. Wait until you see an area that you'd like to add to or change. Ignore the voice that says, "All of it!"
- Simply decide on the one part that needs something different. Then paint or collage as you wish.

You have now reached phase two. Again, don't overthink it. Try to accept what is already there and react to it.

- Give yourself 20 minutes to work on the picture. If you truly have no idea what to do next, then quickly rip little sections out from different pages of the magazines and attach them, covering the parts of the picture you consider most muddy or confusing.
- Keep working. Push yourself forward even if you feel lost.
- Trust your instincts. Logic won't help you here.
- When the 20 minutes is up, lean your piece against the wall and look at it. If you've been working side by side with another person, talk to each other about what you see and what you experienced during the exercise.

Now, if you've decided to go on to phase three and work with a friend...

▸ Swap pieces. Each of you is going to give the other full permission to work on the other's collage. Of course if your working partner is elsewhere, you'll have to make the exchange next time you meet or by mail.

▸ Continue to paint and collage as if the work were yours. You will probably feel detachment, relief, and/or resentment toward me for giving the instruction. That's okay. Do it anyway. You are already pushing your boundaries and finding out about both your art and your resistances. Confusion is merely the last bastion of letting go and allowing the process of creativity to take over.

▸ After you've spent 30 minutes working on what was your partner's piece, switch back. It doesn't matter if you like or dislike what your partner has done. Work into your old picture. Look for the sections you quite like, reshaping the parts that work least. Spend at least another 30 minutes painting, collaging, and experimenting.

Do not be tempted to add 3-D elements. Turning the 2-D surface into a relief brings with it additional confusions.

When you finally come to a halt, take your work somewhere else, somewhere that's uncluttered and where you can really look at it. Is it unbalanced or too symmetrical? Are the colors muddy? Are there too many figurative elements confusing the narrative? Is the piece dynamic or passive, and is that appropriate for the subject matter? Learning to ask the right questions is a big part of developing a picture.

Remember, this isn't your possession, nor is it a glass through which you can project a chosen self-image. Wholehearted art is a mirror, a record of your learning. If you embrace what this picture is trying to tell you, you will have begun a long and ultimately rewarding apprenticeship.

When working on a piece of art, it is always difficult to decide which of the multiplicity of materials and techniques to apply next. So, if the exercise helped you start to grow a picture, please keep in mind that you can always write a whole list of instructions for yourself, cut them up, roll them into small balls, and chuck them into a hat. Then, pick them out at random, following the prompts as you go.

HINT

What you end up with may seem strange, but because it's not contrived, it doesn't have to remain an isolated piece of art; it can equally act as a fresh start and a launching pad for a piece of prose or poetry.

Finishing Lines

The standard way of writing fiction is to plot a story line, then flesh it out as you go along. Once begun, some authors, like Joseph Conrad, would work on one page at a time for eight hours a day. Others, like Georges Simenon, the creator of the French detective Maigret, would spend weeks mentally developing a story line, then explode onto paper with 200 pages in 48 hours.

▶ Their speed may have been vastly different, but their linear approach was similar.

However, that's not the only way to write. I sometimes begin creating a book in the middle or in a series of middles, expanding them outward until they join and the story makes itself known to me.

In some ways it doesn't matter where you start; the key is to get moving so that you have something down on paper to work with. Trying to get everything perfect from the outset can be crippling. You cannot experiment and be flawless at the same time. Better to let first thoughts have their run and then see what comes next.

This next exercise is meant to be a springboard. I'll start you and then you take it from there. There's no guarantee it will blossom into a novel or even a short story, but what matters is that you get under way and don't waste the day staring at a blank page, waiting for inspiration to strike.

Materials: pen and notebook
Time: 30 minutes

INSTRUCTIONS

Add to the following starting points by writing down whatever comes to mind. Don't stop to think – just go with your stream of consciousness.

Complete this sentence: *The horse felt obliged to express itself by...*

When you've done that, write down the sentence that might come before that sentence.

Then compose the sentence that follows the obliged horse sentence.

Now another sentence to finish: *She could not help herself, the date was waiting...*

Same again. Write the preceding sentence and the following one.

And again complete and add the before and after: *Elvira looked at her brother's fast-growing...*

You should now have three sets of three sentences. See if you can find a way to link these sets together in a vaguely cohesive fashion. Once you've done that, you can go back in and edit it, changing a few words here and there to help bring it together. By then it should have some life of its own. Try expanding it further, developing any characters or themes that have begun to show themselves.

Just write – keep going till your 30 minutes are up. Then read it aloud to yourself.

HINT

Even if you don't end up with a story, I hope you get to see how easy it is to begin a piece of writing and that you don't need a big idea to get started.

7 Building a Country

Inside every one of us is a world just as significant as the five-senses world we share with others. This interior landscape is a place of personal mythology that's potentially far more potent than our passing fantasies or daydreams.

Most of us know our day-to-day reality-based environment enough to function reasonably well, but it strikes me how surprisingly few people know their internal universe intimately. And that's a pity because it is the place where creativity begins and individuality flourishes.

With your permission, I'd like to give you some assistance by showing you how to build and develop your internal domain in a way that will help inform, support, and bring the richness of Trickster-mixed color to your creative life.

You are going to be building your own country. Your country is completely how you choose it to be. It can be big or small, fanciful or practical. As you think of it, so it shall be inside you. No one can change it apart from you, and you can change it anytime, any way you wish.

This exercise has a number of parts, and I encourage you to set 3 or 4 hours aside to work on it.

Materials: pen and notebook, blank postcard, paints, and collage stuff
Time: 3 hours minimum
Size: 6" × 4"

INSTRUCTIONS

Part 1:

Write down whatever leaps into your head for each of these questions. You'll have a chance to edit and adapt them later.

Answer one question at a time. Don't read the next question until you've finished responding to the previous, or you'll trip over yourself even before the Trickster sticks his foot out!

1. How big or small is your country?
2. What's your country's geography and terrain like?
3. What kind of climate does it have? Does it vary?
4. How big a population inhabits your country, and what's the makeup?
5. What's the currency? (I suggest you don't choose barter — it precludes the possibility of inventive tender)
6. What are there in the way of animals on land, under water, and in the sky? Can they speak? Do some of them have other qualities or peculiarities?
7. How does your country run politically?

8. What beliefs are held by the people (and possibly the animals)?
9. What does the night sky look like?
10. What else can you say about your country that will make it tangible?
11. What's the name of your country?

Go back and expand on what you've written. If you have created a Utopia, you might find it a bit bland after a while and decide to spice it up with odd joke-telling piranhas or switch your currency from stones to fossilized lychee. It's totally up to you.

Part 2:

Now that you have established your country and it has a name, you are about to commission yourself to design your country's first postage stamp – with name and value. You can paint, draw, or collage it at 200 percent, then have it reduced down to size on a color copier. Cut the rectangle out, and glue it to the back of a used stamp of the appropriate size.

Then, on a 6″ × 4″ blank postcard, using any materials you wish, create an image suitable for your country. On the reverse side, write home, telling the folks back there the thing you like best about your new country.

When that's done, you can glue the postage stamp you just made to your postcard.

Mailing is optional.

Part 3:

Write a short article about your country's history (This backstory will help build a foundation.)

After that, it's up to you. You could expand into anything – from an illustrated encyclopedia of your land's birdlife to a series of folk or fairy tales. Choose whatever makes your country more real for you. The only limit is the restrictions you place on yourself.

As strange as it may seem to some, this country is not a place of daydream and evasion – quite the opposite. It is a means by which we can open the passageway between daily drudgery and the infinite imaginings in our heartland.

HINT

This exercise is not designed to encourage anyone to abdicate from daily reality. The outside world still needs to be lived to the fullest. The intent here is to expand your inner life and then open a dialogue between your everyday and your mythic, so that the creativity born within you can eventually exercise itself for the good of all.

Once your country is under construction, you can wander and explore to your heart's content, and with each step you'll be forcing back the blinkers that shroud your peripheral vision.

41

Composition

Composition is really hard to teach, mainly because balance is innate. Yes, there are mathematical rules of harmony and the golden mean can be measured, but the real acid test is not geometrics—it's purely a matter of whether you can feel the rightness of something in relationship to its surroundings. Do you internally "know" when something is right or when it is just off?

Probably the best way to develop a sense of balance is to practice moving shapes around in a rectangle—constantly checking your internal measuring stick, noting the awkwardness of too much or too little symmetry.

The following exercise is deceptively simple and is best done in silence, with no visual distractions around you. Be aware that the more you concentrate, the more you will benefit from your efforts.

Materials: scissors, old magazines and/or newspapers, 6 squares of white paper, and glue stick
Time: 1 to 5 minutes for each square
Size: 6" × 6" per square

INSTRUCTIONS

Cut out a small stack of letters of different sizes from a magazine. They should be black on a white background. These letters are your design elements.

In the first square, place just one letter. Move it around until you feel happy with its position, then glue it down.

In the second square, place one small and one large letter. Again, move them around until you are happy with the formation, taking your time, then glue.

In the third square, place two large letters and one small letter. One of the letters must touch the edge of the square.

For the fourth square, take a large letter and cut it in half. Place the two halves in the square, touching two opposing edges. Then add a smaller letter to the box.

In the fifth square, place 10 small letters, one medium letter, and one large letter cut in half.

And in the sixth square, create a composition using as many letters as you wish; size is up to you. Do not make words out of the letters, as this will switch the activity to a different part of your brain.

If you enjoyed the Zen-like contemplation of filling these squares, you might like to go on and do a larger version (9″ x 9″ or bigger), maybe using some additional colored letters.

HINT

As you work on these compositions, you will almost certainly find yourself either calmed or agitated. If the latter, observe yourself: Don't give in to the frustration, and don't judge yourself. Keep breathing evenly and see if you can discover what's getting in the way of just doing a simple task well.

Transposing Nouns

Back in the 1920s, the Surrealists developed a number of art and writing games devised to break up predictable thinking patterns. They declared that as society's nature is to herd the mass imagination down predictable lines, the artist's job is to find ways of avoiding those well-worn grooves.

This exercise, among others, springs from the same well as those early Surrealist mind-shuffling techniques. The results can be hilarious, ridiculous, and profound—often all at the same time.

As you do this exercise, let go of the desire to make things reasonable. Let the nonsense flow, then watch as it re-forms into its own left-handed rightness.

Materials: pencil and notebook
Time: 30 minutes

INSTRUCTIONS

Take the book you are currently reading, or any other close at hand,
and open it at random. Select a short paragraph approximately three
or four sentences long, and underline all of the nouns. (I suggest you
do it lightly in pencil so that you can erase the graphite with ease.)

Now pick another, completely different kind of text, whether it be
a magazine or a washing machine manual, and select a similar-sized
paragraph. Repeat the process, underlining all the nouns.

Next, copy the two paragraphs into your notebook, but as you
do so, transpose the nouns from the first paragraph, in the order
in which they appear, to the other paragraph.

Here's an example:

Paragraph 1 (novel):
He hurried through a narrow street of medieval houses, their top
stories jutting out over the road, keeping rain off the walkers below,
until he reached the cobbled quayside. To his left was the river.
The tide was high and the moored boats gyrated violently on slate-
colored water. Gerry's cottage was at the end of the row of houses,
the smallest dwelling, separated from the pub by a narrow road.

Paragraph 2 (artist's diary):

The <u>night</u> was profound. It was impossible to distinguish <u>things</u>, save a powdery <u>phosphorescence</u> close to my <u>head</u>, which strangely perplexed me. I smiled when I thought of the <u>Maori</u> <u>stories</u> about the <u>Tupapaus</u>, the evil <u>spirits</u> which awaken with the <u>darkness</u> to trouble sleeping <u>men</u>. Their <u>realm</u> is in the <u>heart</u> of the <u>mountain</u>, which the <u>forest</u> surrounds with eternal <u>shadows</u>. There it swarms with them, and without cease their <u>legions</u> are increased by the <u>spirits</u> of those who have died.

Once you've transposed the nouns you get these new pararaphs...

Paragraph 1 (altered):

<u>Night</u> hurried through a narrow <u>things</u> of medieval <u>phosphorescence</u>, their top <u>head</u> jutting out over the <u>Maori</u>, keeping <u>stories</u> off the <u>Tupapaus</u> below, until he reached the cobbled <u>spirits</u>. To his left was the <u>darkness</u>. The <u>men</u> was high and the moored <u>realm</u> gyrated violently on slate-colored <u>heart</u>. Gerry's <u>mountain</u> was at the end of the row of <u>forest</u>, the smallest <u>shadows</u>, separated from the <u>legions</u> by a narrow <u>spirits</u>.

Paragraph 2 (altered):

The <u>he</u> was profound. It was impossible to distinguish <u>street</u>, save a powdery <u>houses</u> close to my <u>stories</u>, which strangely perplexed me. I smiled when I thought of the <u>road</u> <u>rain</u> about the <u>walkers</u>, the evil <u>quayside</u> which awaken with the <u>river</u> to trouble sleeping <u>tide</u>.

Their <u>boats</u> is in the <u>water</u> of the <u>cottage</u>, which the <u>houses</u> surrounds with eternal <u>dwelling</u>. There it swarms with them, and without cease their <u>pub</u> are increased by the <u>road</u> of those who have died.

Read both paragraphs out loud. Even with the oddness and things like incorrect plurals, the paragraphs have a curious rhythm.

Now join the two paragraphs and delete any words you don't want. You can correct tenses and plurals and add punctuation, but you can't change the order of the words.

You may get something like this:

Night hurried through narrow medieval phosphorescence, jutting out over the Tupapaus below, until he reached the cobbled spirits. To his left was the darkness. The men were high, and the moored realm gyrated violently on slate-colored hearts. Gerry's mountain was at the end of the row of forest, the smallest shadow separated from the legions by a narrow spirit. It was impossible to distinguish streets, save houses, which strangely perplexed him. He smiled when he thought of the rain—about the walkers, evil quayside, which awakens with the river to trouble sleeping tides. Their boats in the water, the houses surrounded with eternal dwellings. There it swarms with them, increased by those who have died.

 Portrait of the Artist as a Young Man
(Apologies to James Joyce)

This is a self-portrait.

Before I named it Me, this motley creature was a skunk who'd sat
sun-bleaching in a taxidermist's window for more than 40 years.
The watercolor box is very old; I found it in an abandoned basement
in Vancouver. The box came from a small town on the U.S. West Coast
called La Conner.

Who we are is a sum of parts. And each of us has a different interpretation of what those parts add up to.

Materials: things that speak to you from the dark corners of old stores
Time: 1 day
Size: depends on your budget

INSTRUCTIONS

Next time you are in a town with a number of junk shops and cheap antique stores, set yourself a budget (say between $10 and $50), then go looking for things that represent who you are at your core, not what people see when they look at you in passing.

Take your finds home and put them together in whatever way starts to make sense.

HINT

Looking after our exterior aids our self-esteem; appearance also acts as a defining flag to those we wish to encounter. But having met them, how can we communicate who we really are and what we need if we have no idea what we look like inside?

11

Traveling with Archetypes

Within each of us is a cast of many characters, yet we have been taught to listen only to one—the "I."

On the night that I felt my first child kick in his mother's belly, I suffered an insight of seismic proportions. Although I intellectually knew him via the appearance of her swollen stomach, that one kick made him exist. In a millisecond I understood that he was real, that birth was real and death was not a concept. I was mortal, and the knowledge felt like I had suddenly been shown the infinite universe in one single flash. My mind all but shut down in an overwhelming panic attack.

A week later, and still internally jellified, I prized myself from the safety of the house and anxiously set off to see an acupuncturist in the hope of getting some support for my shocked nervous system. When I told him what had happened, he chuckled and said, "Sounds like you had a bit of psychic armor fall off. You need to go home and re-suit."

I don't know how serious he was, but I started to think about the idea of inner self-protection, and the notion dovetailed with the Joseph Campbell material I'd been reading about heroic journeys. Images started marching into my head. In my mind's eye, I saw a motley crew of characters wandering haphazardly beside me as I trudged down a long road.

I admit I wasn't impressed by their general demeanor, so I started to imagine what my perfect traveling companions would be like: a troop of handpicked archetypes rather than alter-ego mercenaries. If I were to conceive this properly, I would need to be surrounded, protected from all angles, nurtured, loved, counseled, guided, and defended.

The standard Jungian model for archetypes tends to come pre-formed (one model for all), but that felt impersonal, and it soon became clear to me that I could shape my archetype companions in a form best suited to my own needs. The more I defined them, the more they grew. They started to form a phalanx around my psyche, shielding me when it felt under attack, feeding my hunger for learning, and alleviating the loneliness of the long road.

Now, it's your turn. Imagine the Trickster has loaned you his hat—you put it on and for a moment you experience what it is to be him. Your eyes sparkle, your mind fills with mischief, and illumination marks the path ahead of you. You turn your head to the left and right, and you see many others moving with you. Focusing on the nearest, he becomes more distinct—he grows larger under the light of your gaze.

This exercise will hopefully help you assemble and focus more closely on your own archetypes, ones that will come to your aid whenever you are floundering or in ill health. They will not take you over, nor are they aspects of a split personality (a common fear)—rather, they will be highly responsible citizens of your being. They are there to help you navigate the aspects of your life that you struggle to cope with, and as long as you feed them, they will be with you throughout your soul's journey.

I'd like to begin by introducing four archetypes: the Warrior, the Lover, the Healer, and the Trickster. (You've met our Universal Trickster, but as yet you may not have become fully conversant with your own personal Trickster.)

Materials: pen and notebook
Time: half a day minimum

INSTRUCTIONS

The Warrior

In your notebook, write down the following questions and then your answers:

- ▸ Which animal do you think represents physical power and strength? Which animal swiftness? And which animal speed of thought and reflex? Imagine these three creatures joining together as one.
- ▸ Who's your favorite warrior from the movies or television, someone who epitomizes your idea of a fearless champion? What is it about this individual that draws you to them?
- ▸ Which person from history stands out as having had the greatest depths of psychological strength and integrity?
- ▸ Who in your life has exhibited the greatest mix of bravery and tenacity?

Now, take all four answers, morph them into one person, and give this warrior an extra superhuman ability. There's always room for improvement, but for the time being this is your Arch Warrior, and he/she/it is there to protect and defend you against anyone or anything that wishes you ill.

Imagine you are walking along a path through a forest and a mean-looking monster steps out in front of you—clearly it wants to chew you up and spit you out. However, your newly built warrior steps between you and your adversary.

Write a paragraph describing first the monster and then how your warrior deals with it.

The Lover

In your notebook, write down the following questions and then your answers:

- ► What are your favorite love songs? For a few minutes (no more), allow yourself to dwell within their memories.
- ► From fiction, who do you think represents the perfect lover?
- ► In real life, who has instilled the most passion within you?
- ► Who has given you the most unconditional love? Pets permitted!
- ► What quality would add to your lover's desirability?

Imagine that your answers were merged, forming a lover who would always be there to tend to your needs, someone to comfort you at times of loneliness. What name would you give this perfect person?

Write a paragraph or two describing an evening spent in the company of your Arch Lover.

The Healer

Healers come in many shapes and forms. Think of a few different types of healers, like physicians, wisewomen, gurus…

- ▸ Make a list of all of the great healers that come to mind from this and other civilizations. When you've finished your list, pick two or three that stand out as being extraordinary. Who has done the most to help heal you?

- ▸ Pick a character from a book, a film, or even TV who symbolizes compassion, wisdom, and the power to heal. For me, Cate Blanchett's Galadriel from *The Lord of the Rings* steps gracefully to the fore.

Bring each of these good people together, making them into one. Give this person a name, then stand your Arch Healer behind you to best protect your back.

Close your eyes and feel the security your healer's presence instills. Write a couple of sentences describing what it might feel like if you had your healer at your shoulder the next time you were dispirited, were unwell, or had to go to the dentist for a root canal.

The Trickster

In your notebook, write down the following questions and then your answers:

- ► Think of a friend or companion who has a twinkle in their eye and never lets you get away with telling yourself white lies.
- ► Which comedian makes you belly laugh?
- ► From fiction, think of your favorite foxy rascal, mischief maker, or slyboots, someone like Puck or the Artful Dodger.
- ► Supposing Alfred Hitchcock was your uncle, what sort of birthday party would he arrange for you?

Morph these answers together, and you have your Trickster. He's a brilliant fool, and he's there to make your journey anything but dull, but don't try to slouch off—he won't let you. Take a paragraph to describe what he looks like, how he dresses, and what he does to wake you up.

You now have four companions in your band, but don't stop there. Continue to build your troop of fellow travelers. Spread them around your interior world in whatever changing formation you need. Call on them and their attributes as they are required. Why not introduce a drummer of poems, a sculptor of words, or a scribe of paint? Let them teach you new ways of seeing, hearing, and making.

HINT

It would be easy to pass this exercise off as arty or flaky or some kind of windy psychobabble. Or you may be flying high and feeling invulnerable, but I'm guessing that there will be a day when you badly need to build or rebuild yourself from the inside out. Maybe then you'll return to the roots of your creativity and this place of personal mythology and see the benefit of breathing life into your waiting archetypes.

59

 Limerick

Even when other types of poetry have fallen from favor, "humorous verse" has always been written, read, and recited. Probably the most endearing and easiest form of humorous poetry on offer is the limerick. First conceived by Edward Lear, the limerick's popularity has continued to multiply since its birth in 1846, partly because it's easy to construct the meter (AABBA) and partly because it's a perfect vehicle for rude ditties. That's not to say limericks have to be bawdy; it's just that many of the best ones are inclined to irreverence.

Now, far be it from me to suggest you start composing smutty verse, but if that's the way it comes off the tip of your pen—who am I to cast the first stone?

Here are a couple of classics, to remind you of their pace and structure:

There was a young man from Darjeeling
Who got on a bus to Ealing
It said on the door
Don't spit on the floor
So he got up and spat on the ceiling.

There was an old man named Ben
Who had a terrible yen
The problem was not

The how, why, or what
But the who and the where and the when.

Limericks are a great way to write poetry without pressure.
The structure is so clear and rhythm so pronounced that it's relatively
easy to add and subtract words in order to work toward a good punch
line (clean or otherwise).

Materials: pen and notebook
Time: 5 to 10 minutes for each poem

INSTRUCTIONS

Complete the following limerick:

There was a young man from…
Who…
When he…
His…
And now…

Then have a second try, using all your own words, but this time
make sure the rhymes are more stretched. For example, words like
Bulgaria and *malaria* or *gerbil* and *herbal*. Always read the lines
aloud – it helps with the cadence. But beware, limericks are addictive.
I recently sent my Spain workshop class this exercise, and they were
still doing it two days later on the bus ride to Ronda.

 First Kiss

There are certain experiences that etch themselves indelibly into our brains—whether we want them there or not! First kisses are inevitably up there on the "memorable moment" list. I've yet to meet someone who can't remember, when you ask, "What was the name of the first person you kissed?"

My first kiss was doubly unforgettable because the sweet girl's name was Penny Tune.

So, in the spirit of nostalgia, who was yours, where did it happen, and what memories does it bring back?

Materials: pen and notebook
Time: 10 minutes for each version

INSTRUCTIONS

Write a paragraph describing your first kiss.

Then write a second version, only this time change the story in any way you want. One of the true joys of fiction is the way it allows us to tinker with what was and make it into what might have been.

And lastly, if you want to go deeper, try writing about something a little more intense—a last kiss.

HINT

Depending on the memory evoked, a last kiss can sometimes be an emotionally powerful subject, so only attempt it if you are prepared to tweak a few heart muscles in the name of producing a strong piece of writing.

A Rant

When it was pointed out that some of my more persistent ranting, on such things as the fashion industry and cell phones, had grown somewhat stale, my wife and I came up with the idea of giving those rants arbitrary numbers, like 37 and 44. These numbers now stand in as short-form substitutes for their more time-consuming and exhausting counterparts.

That's not to say rants are all bad. In fact, dispensing with old rants opens up room for fresh, new, interesting rants.

A good rant can be a healthy way to discharge frustration and allow our compressed psyches a chance to release the weight of everyday irritation. A "good" rant is not repetitive or sloppy or whiny, it's not obvious, and it definitely isn't dull. It is an impassioned plea delivered with humor, perceptiveness, and a healthy pinch of self-mockery.

One of the best rants I ever heard was on the British TV series *Coupling*, where a character was being dragged around a department store by his girlfriend. His girlfriend wanted him to have an opinion about which sofa they should buy, and he suddenly launched into a two-minute diatribe about "the uselessness of cushions." The language was beautifully conceived, ludicrously obsessive, and very funny.

A rant needs to find its moment. It helps if good food and alcohol are involved, and it needs to be delivered while those around are receptive.

It's truly amazing how much artistic energy can be released once everyone has liberated a pet peeve.

For me, easy subjects don't count as rant material. Raging at greedy corporations, callous politicians, racism, sexism, drug and gun peddlers, and even people who drive while texting is not ranting; it is merely articulating a social imperative.

So, what do I consider ranting material?

Where to begin?

At what point did it become not just okay but the norm to make potato chip packages bloated with 90 percent air and 10 percent chips? Why do we put up with it? Why don't we simply go around liberating the air from the bags so the companies that perpetrate this cynical and ridiculous facade get the message that we want chips and not large bags of nothingness?

Materials: pen and notebook

Time: 20 minutes to write the rant, then as long as it takes to perform

INSTRUCTIONS

Write a short list of things that irritate you.

Then make a list of things that really annoy you.

And then create a list of things that fill you with righteous indignation.

Now, given that entertaining rants don't work well if the matter is too heavy, pick one of the subjects off your list and write a rant. Two or three concise paragraphs of hearty venting should do the trick. Make sure your rant is both humorous and over the top. When it's done, call in someone who's near and dear to you (could be the dog), and deliver your rant with all the gusto you can muster.

HINT

The point of this exercise is to help find enthusiastic energy. Most of us are pretty clear when something pisses us off. In fact, outside of love, outrage is one of the easiest emotions to access. If we lace the rant with black humor, it doesn't lead to real anger and therefore frees up energy that can be directed toward other creative outlets.

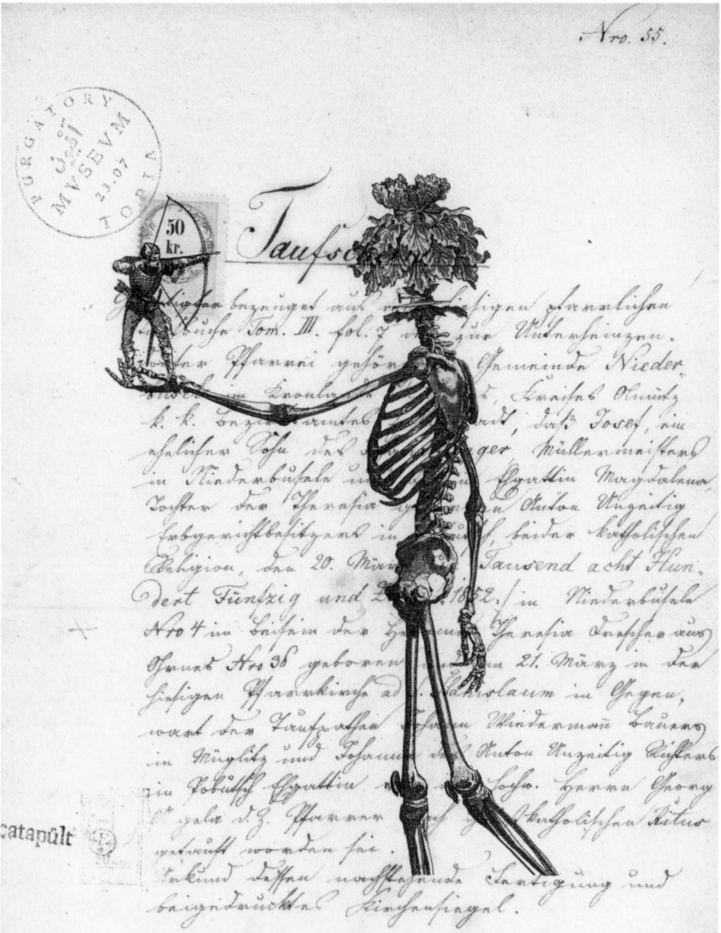
Nro. 55.
PURGATORY MVSEVM
50 kr.
catapült

Inventing Words

In his book *1984*, George Orwell noted that if language shrinks far enough, ideas cannot be communicated and ultimately thinking (for oneself) becomes virtually redundant.

The much-discussed dumbing down of social interaction has led to a shrinking of the average North American vocabulary. And even if an individual goes against the grain and works at expanding their language, it's one thing to be able to articulate and quite another to be understood.

To counter this downward spiral, it helps to exercise our minds by reacquainting ourselves with the incredible diversity of the English language or, better still, coming up with new words.

My favorite escape on long plane flights is inventing words and their definitions. I was on a long haul to Berlin and invented 52 new words and their definitions (twice through the alphabet gobbled up a whole 4 hours). It is surprising how many words the dictionary still needs.

For example: GRINFISH—Anyone (including flight attendants) who smiles constantly or inappropriately.

And PSYCHOSTRATION—Corrosion of the spirit brought about by overexposure to the dehumanizing aspects of progress.

Materials: pen and notebook

Time: 1 hour

INSTRUCTIONS

Write out the alphabet as a column. Then starting at the top, write the first made-up word that comes into your head that begins with the letter A.

Now move on to B and work your way down to Z.

Then go back to the beginning and write a definition for each word you've invented. You can change the spelling if you like.

If you've still got energy once you've worked your way through the list, you can try placing each word in your new lexicon into appropriate sentences.

HINT

Try speaking your new words out loud. If they roll off your tongue, they are more likely to fly.

G R I N F I S H

16 Dice Game

Many's the time I'd be working on a painting, happily driving along, then without being aware of it, I'd turn a corner and suddenly find myself lost. I wouldn't have a clue where to go next. The choices seemed infinite, and I couldn't tell if it was me or the painting that had become agoraphobic. In these cases, the smart thing to do is work on something else for a while, but in my urgency to push forward I'd either overthink myself into the ground or default to tired old solutions.

But then the Trickster taught me to hop sidelong away from headiness or the obvious. Pleased as punch that I'd learned how to guide my brain around the problem, I wanted to explain my new navigational skills to others, but I couldn't fully articulate how I was doing it. Eventually, I realized that I was narrowing down my choices to a few reasonable options so that it didn't matter which one I picked.

Once I understood the process, I started looking for a practical way of jump-starting the hop away from those decision-making impasses. The answer came in the form of tiny old bone dice (I collect them... among many other oddball things). I was placing a die into a Chinese typesetting drawer when I suddenly thought, "CHANCE! Chance is the perfect tool for overcoming the paralysis brought on by too much choice."

mask
quarter
gold
powder
dioxine purple
paint naked
scrape off
dark hooker green
scratch pastel
four inch house brush
take off socks
chrome yellow
silver
spray with toothbrush
fit
rub with both thumbs
drip candle wax
sienna
indian
chinese bristle
red
tear half
raw
ultra marine blue
lamp black
apply with nose
soft squirrel
blot with kitchen cornflake
roundnose brush
mauve
cadmium red medium
fingernail
held
glue on
paper
close eyes
scratch with music
turn upside down
small sable
ppe
tissue
stay
magenta
burnt orange
titanium white
medium filbert
scumble

Materials: 6 pieces of paper of varying sizes and weights, 6 tubes of acrylic paint, 6 paintbrushes of varying sizes and textures, 1 die, and pen and notebook

Time: 1 hour

Size: 12" × 9"

INSTRUCTIONS

Number the pieces of paper from 1 to 6. Throw the die and select the corresponding piece of paper for whichever number comes up.

Then number the tubes of paint, throw the die again, and set the appropriate tube aside. Do the same with the different brushes (small, large, soft, hard).

Now write down six different types of marks you could make, ranging from a single stroke to covering the whole of the paper. Throw the die, and with the color and brush you set aside, make the mark on your paper.

Keep writing lists of six things you might do to your painting. Keep throwing the die and doing what comes up.

Make sure you vary the lists. For example, you could put down five reasonable possibilities and one outrageous one. Or you could put down a whole batch of off-the-wall options, such as (1) take socks off to paint; (2) apply paint with nose; (3) paint for 30 seconds with eyes closed; (4) apply paint with old toothbrush; (5) drip candle wax onto picture; (6) glue cornflakes to picture's surface.

If these suggestions seem a little arbitrary, remember Victor Hugo: a brilliant man who wrote his novels while standing stark naked at the lectern.

Keep coming up with new sets of six options, and remember to take notice of how the focus moves away from trying to control and dominate the painting and toward your imagination. Trust the process, and the art will find itself.

HINT

It's important that you make a firm contract with yourself that you will do whatever the die decrees. If you chicken out, you lose.

Although I've described how to use the die for introducing chance into a painting, this game can just as easily be used for writing, music, or any other art form.

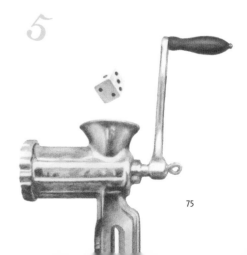

17

Porky Pies or Passionate Lies

While the expression *bum's rush* is usually accredited to early twentieth-century America, its true origin is much older. The word *bum* comes from the German *bummler*, a lazy person who spends their time sitting on their buttocks. The first known mention of the word appeared in a Carmelite tract from 1387 and referred to exhausted praying monks relieving the pressure on their bruised knees by sitting back on their heels. In Italy, during the more forgiving fourteenth century, novices were given rush mats to ease the pain of kneeling through particularly long vigils. However, when one of those novices fell asleep and couldn't be woken, they were ignominiously dragged out of the nave on their rush mats.

Hence the emergence of the term *bummler* or *bum's rush*.

The above is a lie, or to put it more palatably, a "fiction." Tell any story with authority and conviction, and it's liable to be believed. Tell it enough times, and if no one contradicts it, it eventually becomes an implied truth.

Truth and lies are abstractions, and within our minds they are forever being chopped and diced by the distorted needs and preoccupations of our memories. Given time, the distinctions between the tales we tell ourselves and the events we first experienced fade or become misty, and our interpretations no longer hold their original meaning.

Truth declares itself unchanging in a universe where all things change. This being so, truth itself is telling lies.

Those who hold truth so dear that they are unwilling to see its duplicity rarely enjoy the pleasure of storytelling. A good yarn is no more and no less than a passionate porky pie.

If you are going to make something up, then be prepared to give it the full nine yards.

Materials: pen and notebook
Time: 30 minutes

INSTRUCTIONS

Write a paragraph describing an unusual thing that once happened to you.

Now write a second paragraph describing something unusual that didn't happen to you. Make sure this fiction is believable.

Ask yourself which of the two paragraphs you enjoyed writing the most. Your answer will tell you a lot about the way you approach your art form.

This can also become a game with a group of friends or strangers. Each person tells two stories to the group, one true, one false (obviously no one can already know which is which). The group then asks questions about the two events, trying to catch out the storyteller. After the cross-examination, everyone has to guess which is the lie.

HINT

Don't make your fiction a small variation on something that happened to you or someone you know; that's a cop-out. When you are inventing the lie, do it with brazen conviction. You'll have more fun, and your audience will appreciate it all the better.

 Board Game

Anyone who has ever been carried aloft by the great trickster Monty Python knows that there is much sense in nonsense. Monty Python's film *The Meaning of Life* was both profound and preposterous, and in honor of its irreverence and its disregard for all moral certainty and codes of ethics, I'd like to encourage you to create a board game whose theme is also "the meaning of life."

As a kid, my friends and I would often spend an afternoon making up board games. Sometimes they'd be serious attempts to invent a new Monopoly or the like, but quite often they were just plain strange, like Pigs vs. Penguins (one of my less cohesive strategy games). In many ways it was our wacky inventions that gave us the most pleasure.

Leaving reason on vacation, this exercise will require a merciless willingness to engage fully with absurdity. From birth to death, we are subjected to a dizzying maelstrom of confusing events. No matter how hard we strive to overlay reason, life just won't cooperate.

With that in mind, I encourage you to construct your board game so that it reflects both the ridiculousness of existence and the pure exhilaration of our journey.

Please feel free to make your game as general or personal as you wish.

Materials: wooden board, newspaper and magazine clippings, old foreign coins, pictures of houses or people or things, paint, little blocks of wood, small plastic animals, whatever else takes your fancy, paintbrush, and wood glue
Time: 1 hour plus
Size: up to you

INSTRUCTIONS

Using your disparate accumulation of oddments, create your own game board with pieces. Feel free to make it as illogical as you see fit.

Just make sure your grand Meaning of Life game includes everything from philosophy to politics and spirituality to the arts and commerce. Use cards, dice, money, or whatever traditional board game devices you desire in order to play.

Have fun. Keep in mind that it's important to step back far enough to see beyond our day-to-day struggles.

HINT

Many people find it hard to throw off the shackles of sensibleness, or when they do their ideas dissolve into chaos. The trick here is to select everyday things, allow the elements to shuffle into absurdity, then re-order them into their own kind of reconstituted sense.

The Unusual Suspects

Joseph Cornell made shadow boxes out of the discordant remnants of other city dwellers' lives, while Andy Goldsworthy finds objects in the great outdoors that echo and resonate a natural harmony. Different "finders and composers," both are looking for some kind of universality outside themselves. But in order for their works to solidify, they have to pass through the filter of an individual and idiosyncratic viewpoint.

Find a nice box, roughly the size of a shoebox, and walk around your house or apartment loading it with the objects you consider of most personal significance to you. Everything from love letters and family photos to the spoon your dearly departed aunt gave you for Christmas a number of years ago. Once you've done that, set those objects aside.

Keep these treasures, cherish them, but do not try to use them in your art. They are far too precious for you to be objective about. They will inhibit you because you will be attached to protecting the memories within. They have become specific to your perspective, and because of that, you will never be able to see them stripped of their nostalgia. In a couple hundred years, they will have taken on a different persona, though still, like the contents of any cabinet of curiosities, they will inevitably be more history than art.

This exercise will help you develop the individuality of your own selection process without indulging in self or family glorification. Your work will begin to reap the benefits of becoming more significant to others.

Materials: 1 sheet of white paper, and others to be established by circumstance
Time: none
Size: 20" × 10"

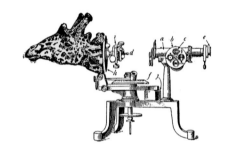

INSTRUCTIONS

Head out into your local trawling zone, be it forest, garage sale, beach, or junk store. Go hunting for things that speak to you. Start small; be a divvy (look it up!).

Bring your finds home and lay them out on a table. Move them around. Start to group them, maybe by material, maybe by shape or color, or maybe by some other more unexpected connection.

When you have a group of five or six, line them up on the sheet of white paper, with a few inches of space between each one. These are your unusual suspects. Photograph the lineup.

Look hard at the photo, absorb the connections from one object to another, and then see how they connect to you. What was it exactly about each object that drew you? Was it the color of the rust, or did the shape of the old can remind you of something you used to play with in your grandpa's garden shed? Our instinctive choices usually have deeper roots.

HINT

Once you get the taste for making connections, you will almost certainly find yourself compelled to trawl further.

Ice and Fire

Are ideas fought for in a "muck-and-bullets," trench-warfare kind of way, or are they given to us by the gods? If we are to believe the latter, and that slivers of genius can be passed through us, then who are we to thank, the Muse or the Duende?

If the Muse, then we are in for a waiting game, for she glides upon the wind and graces us with her gift of creativity only at her whim. She may come tomorrow, but more likely she will leave us stagnating in the doldrums for what may seem like an eternity—and sometimes is.

The Duende, on the other hand, is a fire to be stepped into. It passes up through the soles of our feet and burns within us as a creative passion. We become the channel and the chimney through which the fire rages. It is silent consummation of risk and knowledge. Made visible, it is huge, potent, and patient, but less tolerant than anything the human will can grasp. It is a sweet bliss that will infiltrate the bloodstream and never let us rest.

Materials: 2 wooden boards, paints, and whatever else seems appropriate for the task
Time: half a day for each
Size: 14" × 10"

INSTRUCTIONS

Think of the two boards as giant playing cards.

On one, create an image representing the Muse; on the other, the Duende.

When you have completed them, ask yourself which card you wish to play.

HINT

The Muse is not an angel, and the Duende is no demon. No more than the harpist is from Heaven or the flamenco dancer from Hell.

 Four-Square Collage

One of the regular problems that comes up when working on a free-flowing piece of artwork is the tendency to repeat what we already know and have done many times before. Even though we know there are almost an infinite number of different combinations of marks, shapes, and colors, we tend to revert to the predictable.

In order to get around this form of repetition, we sometimes need to incorporate a little sleight of hand.

Materials: 4 blocks of wood (4″ × 4″ each), acrylic paints, general ephemera, and masking tape
Time: 1 hour
Size: 8″ × 8″

INSTRUCTIONS

Put the 4 blocks together facedown to form an 8" x 8" square. Hold them roughly together with a couple of pieces of masking tape. Flip the square faceup again and start building a quick, unpremeditated collage, gluing down bits of paper and adding paint casually.

Move from chaos to order and back again repeatedly. Make a mess, give it some order, then make a mess again.

After 10 minutes of fervor, stop. Cut the blocks free from each other. That means removing the tape from the back and running a blade horizontally and vertically to release the four 4" x 4" sections. Rearrange the blocks into a totally different 8" x 8" formation. Retape and get back to collaging. In order to reunite the picture, you will need to rework the shapes and colors. Try to see this as a catalyst to a different way of looking.

After another 10 minutes, separate them again and this time rejoin the four blocks as a 4" x 16" picture. From then on, use the blocks in any formation you wish as long as you use all four.

Keep changing the square formations until the hour is up.

HINT

Between each new formation, take two minutes to look at what you've done. This exercise acts literally as a block breaker of personal cliché, while forcing you to deal with change.

Lost in the Forest

In my second year at art college, one of the lecturers decided that our class was becoming a little too wrapped up in art with a capital A, and he decided to take us off into the local forest to do something different.

When we arrived, he told us we were going to make a scaled-down village out of sticks, stones, moss, and anything else we could find. We started to complain that it was childish. But he insisted, and slowly we began collecting bits and pieces. Within five minutes we were all so absorbed with our project that we barely noticed two hours pass.

When he finally called us together, we complained because we didn't want to stop.

He asked us what the afternoon in the forest had taught us about art.

Being 17 and Londoners, our response was, "Dunno."

"I'll tell you," he said. "You have learned to play, and in so doing you have learned the essence of your future craft."

We had no idea how smart he was.

I've re-created this village building "game" a number of times when teaching my workshop in Spain, and on all but one occasion the students took to it like ducks to water.

However, there was one time when it went a tad pear-shaped. I split the group of 12 arbitrarily in half, and they headed out to different parts of the grounds around an old mill. What followed was fascinating.

One group dived in and, without discussion, started to create their village, joining the houses, gardens, ponds, dams, and roads. The other group stood and discussed every tiny detail, arguing about planning permissions and ultimately becoming more and more agitated by each other's interpretations of how to build the model community.

At the end of the allotted time, the two groups met back at base, and we took turns to see the results of their labors. Group one stared on in total amazement when they saw that group two had produced virtually nothing and were clearly up to their ears in frustration with one another. When group two descended to the stream and saw the first group's expansive township, it was easy to read their looks of disappointment at the opportunity they'd missed and how their competitiveness had neutered the experience.

After lunch, we chatted about what had happened, and both groups admitted it was an experience that would stay with them for some time.

If I had tried, I could not have contrived a better way to teach the importance of letting go and allowing oneself to simply be—or, as I am prone to say, to "trust the process."

Thus, in the spirit of my old art teacher, who was fond of quoting Jung—"There is no creativity without play"—I'm going to send you off to play.

Materials: found materials

Time: 2 hours minimum

Size: suggested scale around 10 percent

INSTRUCTIONS

Go out into the garden or park or forest, and build a miniature village out of the things you find there.

At first this wee task may seem trite, and you may sense resistance to doing it, whether it's thinking that the weather isn't great or that the project feels simplistic. Ignore those thoughts. Just have some fun making those houses and roads and bridges and hydro stations.

It's as important an activity as painting a large canvas or carving a marble sculpture because it will remind you what it is to be completely involved in an activity for that activity's sake. So wind, rain, or shine, get your head down and get out there and enjoy yourself like you did when you were eight years old.

HINT

Whether you do this on your own or in a small group, try to make sure your little patch of landscape doesn't have an audience. It's hard to let yourself go if you are being watched.

Jack Yeats, W. B. Yeats's brother, wouldn't let anyone in his studio for sixty years—he said it was the only way he could remain honest.

23
Poetry of Silence

Many years ago, when I was working on *The Ceremony of Innocence*, the CD-ROM version of *Griffin and Sabine*, with Peter Gabriel's Real World Studios, we were coming to the end of the two-year project and were starting to take a broad overview of all of the interactive postcards we'd developed. We realized that without intending to, we'd made the cards progressively more and more about clicking and moving the mouse. In order to get the postcards to switch from the front image to the text on the back, it was necessary to figure out a prescribed sequence of actions. After a long discussion, our design team came up with the idea of making one card that required no action at all in order to get it to flip. If you waited patiently for 30 seconds without touching anything, the card would turn over of its own volition. But if you so much as wiggled the mouse, another 30 seconds was added to the turnover time. We had no idea how hard we were making it for some people!

It was a finger-jabber's nightmare, and we received a ton of letters from 18- to 25-year old men who swore the card had a bug because they couldn't make it work.

We are reared on action and conditioned to feed off our adrenaline. Stillness is a rare commodity. But without calm, we end up a bundle of nerves—desperate for rest and unable to slow down far enough to take what we need. Quiet contemplation and poetry have long been friends,

and of all the poems I've seen, "The Lake Isle of Innisfree" by
W. B. Yeats is the one that never fails to soothe me. Whenever
I read it, I'm reminded of what is real and what is an illusion.

Materials: recording device

Time: around 20 minutes

INSTRUCTIONS

No matter what you use, an old tape machine or Garage Band, make
a recording of the Yeats poem. Please read it yourself (no one else
has to hear it). That's important because it will help you absorb
the words fully. And reading it three or four times, trying to get the
intonation right, will heighten your understanding and allow it to
work its balm.

▶ I've taken the liberty of removing the line breaks in order to make
the poem an easier read.

The Lake Isle of Innisfree

I will arise and go now, and go to Innisfree, And a small cabin build
there, of clay and wattles made: Nine bean-rows will I have there,
a hive for the honeybee, And live alone in the bee-loud glade. And
I shall have some peace there, for peace comes dropping slow, Dropping from the veils of the morning to where the cricket sings; There
midnight's all a glimmer, and noon a purple glow. And evening full

of the linnet's wings. I will arise and go now, for always night and day I hear lake water lapping with low sounds by the shore; While I stand on the roadway, or on the pavements grey, I hear it in the deep heart's core.

HINT

If for whatever reason you don't respond to the Yeats poem, search for something that does work for you. Maybe some Japanese haiku or some Robert Frost?

 Altered Models

When I was creating *The Museum at Purgatory*, I picked up a few plastic action figures from a garage sale, took them back to the studio, and began binding them in cheesecloth and muslin. Then I doused them in coffee and strong black tea. Once they were dry, I dragged them around to the backyard, rubbing moss and paint into them. Little by little they turned into 5,000-year-old miniature mummies. I then wrote an account of how these shrunken mummies had been found in Belshatha, where the translated hieroglyphs had confirmed that even though they were banned in the Old Kingdom, many slaves and animals were mummified and then covertly reduced in order to assist their entry into the afterlife.

The idea here is to do something similar: to radically alter an action figure, doll, or model. You can pick one up for a few cents at a garage sale or junk store if you don't have access to a kids' cupboard of discarded toys. Change it in stages, until it is unrecognizable from its original appearance. You can pretty much do whatever you want in the way of adding and subtracting bits. You can cover it in paint or plaster, re-clothe it, burn it, bejewel it, soak it in beeswax...The sky is the limit.

Transformation is easier than creating from scratch and feels like a kind of alchemical manipulation that's fascinating to observe.

Materials: doll or action figure, cheesecloth, anything that can be used to create a transmogrification, and pen and note card

Time: 1 to 2 hours

Size: roughly 10 inches high

INSTRUCTIONS

Do whatever you can to change the figure. The idea is to give it a new life. And as it grows, imagine how it came to be like this, as if time, and not you, were forming it.

Do not decide beforehand what you want it to look like. Let it alter with your assistance rather than with your command. The best work comes when you don't know what you are doing.

After you have finished reinventing your doll, which may have become transformed into anything from a steampunk goddess to a charred religious relic, take a further 10 minutes and write up a museum card describing the imagined origins of your new doll/object. It's fascinating how these fake official descriptions can add justification and give credibility to your constructions.

HINT

When is any piece finished? As you near the end of a work, it grows less noisy, no longer demanding that you change this or that.
Then, after its whispers have ceased and it is silent, it is complete.

 Face Collage

Giuseppe Arcimboldo was an Italian painter born around 1527 who painted imaginary portraits of figures whose heads were made up solely of things such as fruit and vegetables or fish.

Even to this day his pictures are quite bizarre. And in the half a millennium since then, we never seem to tire of playing with faces. From plastic surgery to Frankenstein's monster, making faces – even the expression has connotations of distortion – provides us with seemingly limitless fascination.

There are two parts to this collage exercise. The first is relatively straightforward, and the second requires a tad more ingenuity.

Materials: old magazines or old picture books, 2 pieces posterboard, matte medium and brush, and paint (optional)
Time: 45 minutes
Size: 9″ × 12″ each

INSTRUCTIONS

Part 1:

From any source or sources, locate at least five or six different faces (they could be human and/or animal); tear out the noses, eyes, mouths, hair, etc.; and pile them up. Then create a collaged face, constructing it from the various bits in your pile. Don't fret about symmetry; in fact, the outcome will probably be more interesting if the face is asymmetrical.

Part 2:

This is where Mr. Arcimboldo comes in.

Again using magazine tear-outs, build a face, but this time create it out of anything other than body parts.

Once you've finished the two collages, you can add paint if you wish to bind the elements more tightly together.

HINT

The history of art as seen through coffee-table books can be misleading. The world's museums hold many strange and curious paintings that never see print, while some paintings have lost almost all meaning through overexposure. Next time you are in a city other than your own, try to find out if the city museum or gallery has an annex or a back room that houses the "lesser works," and see if they'll let you view them.

26 Chiaroscuro

Imagine you are in total darkness, then in a space so full of light it's devoid of any shade and shadow. As opposite as these two states are, the experience is very similar—there is nothing to see. Light and dark need each other in order to exist.

Chiaroscuro is this relationship between light and dark, and the shaping effect they have on each other. When both white and black are present on a surface, the white appears to be closer to us than the black is. The illusion is created that a picture has depth. A white mark on black paper becomes a light source. A black mark on white paper makes a hole. The control and modification of this chiaroscuro allows the artist to trick our eyes into thinking 2-D is really 3-D.

Black-and-white drawings, photographs, and movies have all taken a backseat to color, and that means our modern eyes have very little experience with chiaroscuro, and we often struggle to understand what we are looking at. Add to this another set of illusions we have to deal with: warm colors like red appearing to come forward, and cold colors like blue seeming to recede. What does the eye do when it sees a dark red next to a light blue? Which comes forward, and which goes back? It's confusing and the truth is, the answer depends on the circumstances.

If we are to understand how a beast moves, we need to look at its skeleton. If you want to learn to really see, you'll need to set color aside for just a short while. Take a look at a book of good black-and-white photos. Notice exactly how your eye travels in and out of the shadows. Do the same with an old movie. You don't have to watch it all (unless you can't help yourself) – 10 minutes of something like *Casablanca* should do for a start.

Once you've done that, try this exercise.

Materials: 1 sheet of strong white paper, stick of compressed charcoal, some regular willow charcoal, kneaded eraser (aka putty rubber), and fistful of cheap, crustless white bread rolled into a ball
Time: start with 40 minutes… see how it goes
Size: roughly 36" x 24"

INSTRUCTIONS

This is going to be messy. Wear old clothes and protect the floor if you don't want it showered in charcoal dust.

With the stick of compressed charcoal held on its side, cover the paper. Rub the black into the surface of the paper until all white has gone. Blow the excess charcoal dust off your drawing.

Now, first with the bread wad and then with the kneaded eraser, start cleaning sections here and there so that the white paper reappears. Both the bread and the eraser will quickly saturate with charcoal, but you can keep using them if you bend or break them to expose their clean interiors. The white of the paper will never be fully white again, but by comparison it will seem that way.

Alternate drawing with the charcoal and removing with the bread ball and eraser. Very soon you'll see that you are shaping your picture from front to back as well as from side to side. Keep going until it feels more like sculpting than drawing.

It's up to you whether you wish to make your drawing abstract or figurative or something somewhere between the two.

HINT

You fear the dark and so you try to banish it with light, yet all you do is lose your sense of balance.

—The Trickster's Lament

 Form and Content

Because form and content are usually entwined and because we normally don't need to separate them, we rarely stand back and ask ourselves, "Which of the two do we consider more important?"

When I started teaching workshops, I thought I would bring the question into focus by setting up an exercise that pitted figurative art against abstract art. But there's too much blur in the middle, and it soon became as confusing to me as it was to the class. Then I tried getting students to make two piles of images torn from magazines: one containing interesting scenes or subjects, namely the "things" that caught their attention; the other containing no recognizable objects, just interesting sections of color and shape. This was less confusing; people were seeing what I was getting at intellectually, but it still wasn't getting through in a form that was altering their way of seeing.

In the end, I decided to use words instead of pictures and created the following little exercise.

Materials: pen and notebook
Time: 10 minutes

INSTRUCTIONS

Pick 12 words you like. Write them down as soon as they pop into your head; don't second-guess yourself. Then split the words into two columns. The first should be words that have pleasing associations, like "Parisian" or "coffee"; the second should be words you picked because you liked either their sound on your tongue or their aesthetic appearance when written, such as "cantankerous" or "scaramouche."

If you have more words in column one than in column two, your painting choices will be more content driven; conversely, if the other column is longer, aesthetics are more your driving force.

HINT

Sometimes you have to switch brain sides to access your agenda. Use images to provoke logic, and words to stimulate the visual.

 Mundane vs. Romantic

A reporter once asked me if I was romantic, to which I glibly replied, "No, I'm a failed cynic." What I was attempting to say was that, in my youth, I treated the best attempts of humankind to rise above greed and ignorance with contempt. I would announce, to those who would listen, that dreamers were fools and that any attempt to redirect our crocodile nature was doomed to failure.

Mostly I thought it cool to be cynical. However, the pose wore thin, and I realized I liked life and people too much to keep wearing the dark glasses. So I embraced the role of the romantic and traveled the country reading my stories and being a generally cheerful fellow.

And then dusk began to fall in the shape of exhaustion, taxes, publishing demands, and divorce, and it became tougher to maintain a romantic view of things. I oscillated between the light and the dark.

Now, I seem to have found a happy medium. I live on the cusp, balancing my cynical and romantic sides, accepting my obligations and acknowledging the need for homeopathic doses of libertine.

Materials: assortment of art supplies
Time: 2 hours
Size: anywhere between 3" and 3'

INSTRUCTIONS

Part 1:

Draw, collage, paint, or make an object that represents your sense
of "obligation and responsibility" – the sensible *shoulds* and *oughts*
that we have agreed to uphold, either implicitly or by specific promise.

Part 2:

Now using the same kinds of materials, create an object that represents
liberation from those ties, something that symbolizes the half-dreamed
desire of a less bound-up life.

HINT

My intent is not to make you miserable and desert your loved ones
but to acknowledge a buried yearning and honor it without being
compelled to live it out.

 Graphic Quotes

Profound quotes abound.

Sift through any of the large books and websites dedicated to quotations and see how many hundreds of thousands of wise words have been uttered. If only we could stay in the right frame of mind, these great insights could probably redirect us toward a better way of being. Yet, for one reason or another, we rarely are in a space where profundity truly sticks to our ribs.

Being human, the quotes that tend to stay with us are more likely to be the sharp and cutting ones, the witty retorts, and the studied insults. The great protagonists of the barbed quote knew how to puncture pomposity or slice through the ridiculous: Oscar Wilde, Dorothy Parker, Winston Churchill—each of them a Trickster's familiar. They couldn't help themselves. They'd see a fat balloon and out would come the pin...

Brilliant bittersweet quotes are born to be played with, unlike their more serious brothers and sisters, which seem to lose their meaningfulness when stuck in a frame and hung on the kitchen wall.

Materials: pen, paper, magazine clippings, scissors, and glue stick
Time: approximately 1 hour

INSTRUCTIONS

Poke around. Unearth a pithy quote that makes you laugh and think at the same time.

The object of this exercise is to make your selected quote more graphically arresting.

That means playing with the size and coloring of the words and lettering, and adding images if you wish. It doesn't matter whether you turn it into a graphic poster or a piece of concrete poetry so long as you are using both sides of your brain while you are doing it. And that's achieved when you shuffle image and word.

HINT

Here are a few pointy quotes to get your juices going:

I wouldn't have seen it if I hadn't believed it.
—*Marshall McLuhan*

This is not a novel to be tossed aside lightly. It should be thrown with great force.
—*Dorothy Parker*

If all the economists were laid end to end, they would not reach a conclusion.
—*George Bernard Shaw*

I love mankind; it's people I can't stand.
— *Charles Schultz*

A great many people think they are thinking when
they are merely rearranging their prejudices.
— *William James*

The only sin is mediocrity.
— *Martha Graham*

Always forgive your enemies — nothing annoys them more.
— *Oscar Wilde*

"Sir, if you were my husband, I'd poison your coffee."
"Madam, if I were your husband, I'd drink it."
— *Winston Churchill*

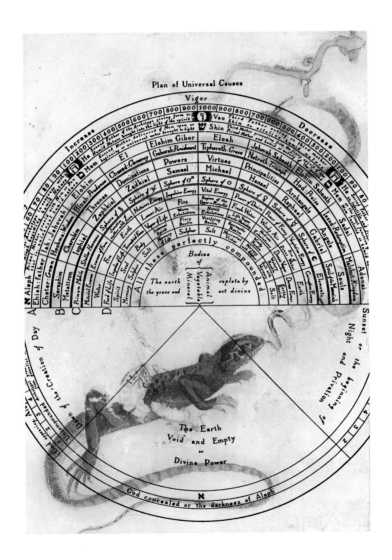

Plan of Universal Causes

The Earth
Void and Empty
or
Divine Power

God concealed or the darkness of Aleph

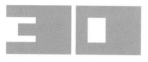

A Marriage of Opposites

A tightrope walker tilts his pole slightly to the left to correct a lean to the right. A tree branch changes direction in order to spread the load. Balance is not a fixed position; it is a state of adjustment. A pendulum swings from left to right and back again. To keep our equilibrium, we need to be able to move from left brain to right brain and back again.

Get stuck on one side or the other, and you will topple over. Of course, if you live among a tribe of toppled people, doing everything from a prone position might seem quite normal.

Part of the Trickster's role is to teach balance. If he sees you leaning too far one way or the other, he's liable to give you a correcting push. Don't fight him. He's trying to help you stand on your own two feet.

In alchemy, when left and right are in harmony, it is said to be a chemical wedding. When word and picture marry, the left and right sides of the brain operate as a unit, and a means of expression is available to us that's far more than the limited view of existence one-sidedness offers.

It is essential that we educate and wed the two sides of our brain if we are to move beyond our tendency to become defensive and bigoted.

If you see a picture of a fish and underneath it there's a sign saying, "Table lamp," you can choose to dismiss it as being incorrectly labeled or you can ask, "Why is that fish called a table lamp?"

There is no definitive answer, that's not the point. The point is to activate the messenger service between your word brain and your image brain, thus bringing you back into an upright position.

Usually I'd counsel against adding easily readable text to a picture, because it dominates the way the image is perceived. We are inclined to read the words and believe they are the interpretation of the picture, and this will often override the more ambiguous content of the image itself. But in this case, I want you to try alternating images and words so that your left and right halves get used to living in equality.

Materials: old newspaper or magazine, scissors, used postage stamps, paper strip, and glue stick

Time: 15 minutes

Size: approximately 2" × 24"

INSTRUCTIONS

Cut out about 20 individual words from a newspaper or magazine and roughly the same number of little images from the same or a different source. Used postage stamps are a good source of small images.

From your image pile, pick one image and glue it to the far left of your paper strip. Switch to the word pile, pick a word, and glue that to the immediate right of your first picture. Then return to the image pile, select a picture, and glue it down. Continue alternately putting down words and images. Don't be too literal; this is not a narrative—not of the premeditated kind, anyway.

Keep going till you've used up all the words and images.

Now here's the tricky bit: Stretch out your strip of paper and try reading it, images and words, as a single message.

HINT

You won't be able to do this unless you locate a point midway between your two hemispheres.

Don't worry if the images and words keep separating. It takes a lot of practice to balance on a high wire.

123

 Learning from Others

Picasso (always the Trickster's apprentice) once said that when it came to painting, he'd steal from anyone but himself. I'm guessing he meant that he needed to be constantly moving within his art and that if he stopped to worry where an idea originated, he would never incorporate it into his visual vocabulary.

I believe that if an artist fails to keep broadening his or her inventiveness, then apathy and repetition will set in. To produce one piece after another that are mere variations on a theme may suit gallery owners, critics, and museums because it makes it easier for them to promote and sell a product, but it does little to stimulate humanity. Young artists who limit their imaginations are in danger of being dishonest to themselves and their audience. Our job as creative individuals is to acknowledge, develop, and shine light on all realities, whether they be concrete or mythological—not for individual glory but because it feeds the collective unconscious and gives permission to others to widen the periphery of their vision.

To copy another person's work without trying to understand and reinvent it is plagiarism. But to imbibe it, reconstitute it, and breathe a fresh life into it, that's different. That's how we learn and grow. The Impressionists were strongly influenced by Japanese woodcuts, the Cubists by African masks; everywhere you look through the history of art there are artists learning from others by observation and interpretation.

Nature is without a doubt the best teacher, but there are others, and many of them can be found in the museums that house the best that all our various civilizations have produced.

Materials: pencil, drawing paper, and anything else of your choosing
Time: 2 hours minimum

INSTRUCTIONS

Pick a painting, a sculpture, or any artifact that you think is sublime or just damned interesting. Study it, in real life if you can, but if that's not possible, then in reproduction.

Start by drawing it. Doesn't matter if you think you can draw or not. The point is to look at it and translate your looking onto paper.

Ask yourself, "Why this piece? What's in its essence that speaks to me?"

Now start a new work. It could be a painting, a piece of writing, or maybe music; just make sure that it starts from that place inside you that was initially transfixed. Push this new work outward, away from the original and toward something different, something intrinsically personal.

For example, you could begin with one of Degas's bronze sculptures of a young ballet dancer. Study and copy it, go to a dance studio and film the dancers, compose some music to go with the dance, then write a play that includes a dance scene.

That's a tall order, I agree, but the idea here is not to limit yourself or prejudge where your creativity might take you.

HINT

There's nothing wrong with starting with a Rembrandt and ending with a Pollock as long as you work through the stages in between.

 Magical Object

The age of science assures us that the darkness of superstition has been driven back by logic and the lightbulb, that organization will quantify and defeat all things unknown.

And while it is undeniably true that so much has been gained in many areas, with all that pigeonholing progress, we have lost some of the "magic."

Magic is as mercurial as love and art, defying definition and exciting us in a way that the science of reason cannot. To some the term is a threat, to others an excuse to indulge. For me, it represents the dawn and the dusk and the other subtleties that an unerring searchlight will bleach white.

No, I'm not offering spells and incantations, merely a homeopathic taste of what it might feel like to create something magical—not something that does magic but an object or artifact that conjures up the essence of unreasonable specialness.

Materials: anything you can get your hands on
Time: 1 to 2 hours
Size: Somewhere between 9" and 24" high

INSTRUCTIONS

Using materials culled from all corners of
your house and garden, make one of the
following: a shrine, a talisman, a wand,
a totem, a charm, a mojo, or any other
thingy imbued with whatever you consider magical. Take this seriously; try to
invest it with all the contrary qualities
you can muster. And when you're done,
be proud of it and keep it somewhere
safe so that you can remind yourself what
magic looks and feels like for you.

HINT

If it makes it easier, replace the word
magical with *spiritual*.

The Unexpected

An Irish navvy living in London goes to a building site looking for work.

He locates the foreman and says, "I'd like a job, please."

Hearing the man's accent, the foreman says, "Piss off, you Irish are all bleedin' thick."

The navvy, being somewhat offended, responds, "I'm not t'ick."

"Yes, you bleedin' are," says the foreman. "You can't even tell the difference between a joist and a girder."

The navvy thinks for a second and then replies, "Yes, I can. Joist wrote *Ulysses*, and Girder wrote *Faust*."

What makes this joke different from the run of the mill is the way it appears to be feeding a stereotypical racist gag and then, with a flick of its tail, turns around and mocks the ignorance of the prejudiced.

Materials: pen and notebook

Time: 1 day to listen and wait for a moment of inspiration, plus 30 minutes to write and refine

INSTRUCTIONS

Like songwriting, joke writing is a special skill. But you won't know if you have it till you try. Hence, your task is to write a joke... that ends in a moral.

How the hell do I do that? I hear you ask.

Start by opening your ears to the things going on around you, snippets of conversation heard in passing. Sooner or later someone is going to say something that sparks a humorous story line. Play with the words, crafting them until you have the body of a pithy joke. Then look for a punch line that twists the tail and makes the listener smile with the irony.

I'm not suggesting it's easy, but with practice you can do it.

HINT

You can never go too far wrong in mocking your own prejudices and obsessions.

 Envelope

Before I began writing from Griffin's and Sabine's shoes, I'd never thought much about envelopes.

I hadn't noticed how damnably clever they were. A kite-like piece of paper that folds into a container—maybe not as sophisticated as an origami crane but brilliant in its own way.

Sadly, from my perspective, the proliferation of email has meant that fewer and fewer personal letters are sent each year. Yet still, when a well-dressed envelope comes tripping through the mail slot, most of us still get a palpable tingle.

Materials: envelope, map or interesting piece of printed paper as large as the envelope when unfolded, pencil, scissors, ruler, glue stick, stamps, and old magazines
Time: 1 hour minimum
Size: depends on your envelope's wingspan

INSTRUCTIONS

Find a smallish envelope with pleasing proportions, then open it up.

This is your template. Lay it over your map or printed paper, draw around the edges, and then cut it out. Score the fold lines creating the front rectangle. Fold and adhere bottom and side flaps with a glue stick.

Select someone to send the letter to – maybe someone you'd like to reestablish contact with or a close friend you share emails with but never communicate with through the mail. Handwrite or type (if you can find an old typewriter, it adds to the flavor) your friend's address onto a thin piece of paper, then cut it out and glue it onto the front of the envelope. Add some good-looking stamps and start thinking about contents.

If you are comfortable writing a letter, do so, but if you're not, then just fill the envelope with a small mix of magazine clippings that visually express your thoughts and feelings. It's surprising how directly images speak.

And if you are feeling truly expansive, you could make the envelope out of a piece of your own artwork and even illustrate the letter with a drawing or collage.

HINT

If you can't think of someone to send it to, send it to yourself. That's how I started, and see what trouble it got me into!

Drawing Empty

When I was 16 and first at art college, I was incapable of drawing anything in proportion.

We spent most of our opening term in the life room, and while we had great teachers and I loved being there, my inability to conquer the basics was starting to drive me nuts. Then came a two-week vacation during which I sheepishly admit I ignored all my studies. Returning to the life room, I expected yet another round of ham-fisted struggling; however, that was not the case. Instead, as soon as I picked up a pencil, it felt different in my hand—it felt somehow like it was an extension of my fingers. And as I drew, the marks I made on the paper immediately started to approximate the model in front of me. I was ecstatic but confused. How could this be? Had a wand been waved over my head during the break, rendering me the power to render?

Only later did I understand that the answer was a little less magical. During the two weeks away, the information I'd previously absorbed had had time to settle and percolate. The part of my brain that had been obsessively trying to direct my hand-eye coordination had finally given up, leaving my center (the balancing device below the heart and above the belly) to deal with what it handles best.

Learning to draw is not just a matter of learning technique, it's about learning to see and letting the retinal images pass through your intuitive grasp of nature's structural rules, so that your fingers know when to move the pencil up, down, left, or right.

Anyone who has tried to assemble a piece of furniture from an instruction sheet, translated from Urdu and composed by a dyslexic Scandinavian sadist, knows what panic is. I've noticed that as soon as the word *drawing* gets mentioned, many people take on a similar look of petrified hopelessness. Unlike the aforementioned unjoinable joinery, there are obvious reasons why drawing has become such a daunting challenge. Quite simply, the art of seeing is seldom taught in schools. Drawing has pretty much been deemed a redundant activity unless an individual is "artistic" and headed for art college.

I cannot overcome anyone's fear of drawing—a fear that was probably fixed in the first instant by a combination of exercises in telegraph-pole perspective and enforced by periods of sitting in front of a bowl of fruit, waiting for it to transmogrify itself onto paper. Instead, in Trickster style, I'm going to try to stimulate those who want to play.

Because many new artists feel embarrassed about "not being able to draw," they turn to other less "intimidating" mediums in the hope of gathering new techniques they believe will disguise the fact that they haven't learned the basic language of seeing. This is harsh, I admit. And I say it only to see if it resonates with you. Look at a tree branch, see the way it grows from the trunk, first left then right, up then down, each change of direction perfectly proportioned.

Now draw a line. See if you can feel (without thinking) which way it needs to travel. If you cannot do that yet, then you still have work to do.

Drawing is not essential to making art, but knowing that a pencil is a friend and not an enemy will allow you to function as an artist without having one hand tied behind your back.

Materials: pocket sketchbook, like a Moleskin; mechanical pencil with a B graphite lead; and kneaded eraser
Time: 10 minutes every day for 1 month

INSTRUCTIONS

Each day start a new page. Draw solidly for five minutes, looking at anything your eye alights on but not looking at the page. Then, refocus on the page and spend five minutes drawing into the marks you've already created. Don't try to represent anything—just play with the lines, letting them evolve as darker masses contrasting against the light of the paper. Watch the shapes come and go. Don't impose any responsibility on yourself.

As for the kneaded eraser, squeeze it to a point so that you can use it to make light marks out of dark areas. Do not use it for rubbing away areas you don't like. If you aren't pleased with a section, keep working into it. At first you'll possibly think you're making a mess, but that's fine. Once you've completed a week's worth of drawings, you'll find yourself more comfortable with letting your eye guide your hand. And all being well, you'll start to see more clearly.

HINT

Next time you are in a museum that houses some good pencil drawings, look at them very carefully. Ignore the subject matter and its representation. Instead, look at the marks, the flow, and the pressure placed on the lines. See the way the pencil has run; in your mind's eye, trace those lines. Absorb through your gut both the marks and the spaces left between them. Absorb it all.

 Sage

A few years ago my friend Shannon Wray and I conceived the idea of inventing a sort of web-based Zen-surrealist *I Ching* oracle. Tickled by our own distorted sense of humor, we deemed it a good idea to name it *Sage* and came up with 99 "big" questions to ask, like, "Is there any worth to a duty born out of enslavement?" Then we came up with 99 ambiguous answers, such as, "Two blue flames are racing up and down the lake's surface. Brilliant words make everything clear."

The idea was that when you clicked blindly on a question tile, it flipped over, and then when you hit an answer tile, it did the same. However, there was no predetermined link, and thus the relationship between question and answer was random and different every time.

We thought this was funny.

Then we wrote a bogus but believable history, describing how *Sage* was discovered in 1914 when 63 goat-vellum scrolls were unearthed in northern Turkey.

We launched *Sage* on my website and waited for people to appreciate our joke.

The appreciation for our distorted humor never came, because the oracle actually appeared to work.

It turned out that no matter how many times you consulted *Sage*, the question was always relevant and the answer always made an obscure kind of sense... the "sense" in *nonsense*.

It seems that the collective unconscious refuses to be teased and that the universe has its own way of mocking our sad shortsightedness. For this, and for all the other ways in which the Trickster teaches us to be humble, I am repeatedly grateful.

Materials: pen and notebook
Time: approximately 30 minutes

INSTRUCTIONS

Write a list of your seven favorite songs. Sing a bit of each song in your head, then pick a line or verse from each song and write it down.

Number the lines from 1 to 7 in the order you thought of them. Set them aside.

Now, imagine that you are woken in the night by a gray-eyed angel and taken to the Oracle at Delphi. As you stand before the Oracle, you are told you will be permitted seven questions. The angel counsels you that it is advisable to avoid asking anything overtly material, like, "How can I make a million bucks?" or too overreaching, like, "What's the meaning of life?"

What are the seven questions you ask? Write them down.

Return to your song lines. These are the answers to your questions. I know, that's a bit weird, but you now need to match them up. The matches will inevitably be a bit surreal, but do your best to find connections.

Now pick the question and answer that seem to fit best and make the most sense.

If the story were true and the Oracle had given this answer to this question, what would it be telling you about yourself? Write that down.

The purpose: The Oracle is inside all of us, and it mirrors back what we already know but cannot see because we are busy being practical. But if we use art and imagination and are willing to wander, we can glimpse reflections of our smarter selves.

HINT

In the words of the diminutive Spanish philosopher Manuel on *Fawlty Towers*, "I know nothing."

143

 Dreams

We may not remember our dreams, but regardless of our age or our country, we all dream. Imagine all the billions of people (and many animals too) dreaming for 7 or 8 hours a day. Consider how many neuron-flashing images and symbols that represents in just a 24-hour period. It's beyond mind-boggling. And yet most of us pay little or no heed to this extraordinary activity. We don't think about what we are doing for a third of our lives. To me that seems nuts.

When I say think about dreams, I don't mean attempt to interpret them; I mean that we should just think about what dreams are and what they actually do in terms of the big picture. And what better time than now? After all, this book is about releasing creativity, and where are we more creative in our lives than in our dreams? There has to be a reason for this torrential outpouring of surreal imaginings.

This exercise comes in two parts. In the first part, you'll find a list of provocative thoughts about dreaming, and I want you to decide which you think are viable and which are nonsense. The second part is about the power of dreams.

Remember, dreaming and creativity run on parallel tracks—if you are driving one train, then the Trickster will be driving the other.

Materials: pen and notebook
Time: as long as you wish

INSTRUCTIONS

Part 1:

If you haven't expended much energy thinking about dreams and dreaming, the following list is going to seem a bit dense, so take your time and read it a few times. After mulling through it all, write down 3 of the points you find most interesting, then try adding a few thoughts of your own.

> ► What if dreaming is a language of communication not designed to be translated into words because it's intuitive and a means of thinking via pictures?
> ► Are dreams private, or might it be possible for other people to see our dreams on another channel, as it were?
> ► Is all the information we glean during daylight being fed through our night dreams into the collective unconscious? And if so, does that collective reward us with information that's been gathered by *all* dreamers?

- Once, when I was going through a period of confusion, I went to sleep in bad need of encouragement. I dreamed of 3 frogs croaking, "Rivet, rivet, rivet." When I awoke, I felt sure there was some instruction in my dream, but I couldn't fathom it. Then it dawned on me: "rivets" was an anagram of "strive." Could it be that the words in our dreams play a code game with us, or is that just too far-fetched?

- Have you ever noticed that dreams respond to observation by becoming even more elusive? If we try to capture, examine, and analyze our dreams, are we simply sticking specimen pins through the Wings of Psyche, inhibiting her capacity to fly?

- Can the Zen-like way in which dreams tease and toy with our intellect be merely a coincidence, or are we being advised by the universe to seek self-understanding?

- Does our commitment (as a society) to a single, colluded reality, where each person is separate yet supposedly perceiving the same world, make us fearful of dreams? Why else would we have downgraded our regard for the dreamworld to that of a low-grade horoscope in a daily paper?

- And… do we have dreams? Or do dreams have us?

Part 2:

Dreams come in all weights and magnitudes, from the slight to the immensely powerful. Think of a powerful dream you once had. It could be recent or when you were younger. Choose one that you couldn't shake off even when you were fully awake. Write it down in as much detail as you can muster.

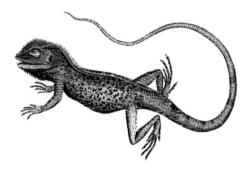

○ Direct transcriptions of dreams rarely work well as art. Think how often you've seen a movie and found a dream sequence weak and ineffective; likewise with writing, dreams retold in fiction usually seem seem too far removed from the story thread to advance the plot. The Trickster is not going to let the artist get away with anything so direct. But when I ask you to put your dream down on paper, it isn't to create art; it's to manifest it in a form that you can walk around and observe from all angles.

Examine your dream as you might an unexpected feeling that's just popped into your chest. Ponder over the images, and imagine yourself to be each of the dream's parts, not just the viewer. For example, if there is a cat padding down the street, try to see your dream through the cat's eyes.

The dream you had may be old, but its contents belong to your subconscious's cabinet of curiosities and will continue to have meaning within its DNA.

Wander around it as you would a marvelous old city and then write more—record all the details and sensations you took little or no notice of the first time around.

HINT

There is a prevalent fashion that says, "Don't bother to think about anything remotely philosophical because old men have already done all the thinking."

It doesn't matter how many books have been written, or how many studies made; each of us still needs to think things through for ourselves. Context is constantly changing; each of us is profoundly different. Never, never stop trying to find your own way of looking at things. Just as dream images reflect off one another in an infinite series of changing patterns and codes, so do our thoughts spiral, constantly attempting to add new configurations to the collective consciousness.

 Top Fives

In the movie *High Fidelity*, the two main characters, who work in a record store, distract themselves by coming up with lists of their favorite top fives — top five dead drummers, etc.

The game fascinated me, and I started making my own lists of things, like top five villainous foreign names that would look good in neon over a nightclub, or top 5 misheard song lyrics, such as, "She'll have fun fun fun till her daddy takes her tea bag away."

One day, while looking through a large art book, I got the idea of making a list of the top five pieces of art I'd steal if I were that way inclined. The list kept changing, but as I added and crossed off some of the world's great treasures, I realized that it was becoming not only a gathering of my artistic taste but a barometer of what I feel is worthwhile and meaningful to me.

Here's the list I ended up with:

Top Five Art Objects I'd Steal If I Could

- ► Da Vinci's sketchbooks
- ► William Turner, any one of his later big paintings from the Tate Gallery
- ► Vermeer's *Girl with a Pearl Earring*
- ► The British Museum's limestone sculpture of Horus (the falcon)
- ► The Alhambra (all of it!)

What started out as a game became a way of focusing my aspirations. The things I picked to purloin represented the ideals of my own art. These ideals were too ephemeral for me to grasp fully but were, nonetheless, signposts of intent—each wrapped in the wistful clarity that comes when seeing a work and knowing its creator(s) refuse to be limited by mere mortality.

Materials: pen and notebook
Time: a few minutes and/or a few days

INSTRUCTIONS

Write a list of your top five most desirable artifacts from anywhere in the world. Then describe what it is about each of them that so draws you in.

HINT

This isn't about wanting and possessing, it's about understanding your passions and using that understanding to direct yourself toward those things that represent significance.

 Blue

Blue is the color of air and historically the rarest of pigments. When we use the word *blue*, we assume other people know what we mean, but the difference between a cool turquoise blue and a warm lilac blue is massive. If we really wanted to describe any given blue, we would need words like *blue-green* or *blue-purple*. By putting two adjacent colors together, we can communicate more clearly. The stronger color leads, the influencing color follows. Flip *blue-green* and you get *green-blue*— again, it's much more descriptive.

Not everyone needs to be precise about colors, but it would help if the words were dictionary ready when they are needed. From what I've been told, before 1900, the Japanese language had no word for what we call *blue*. Colors were broken down in roughly the way I just described.

Materials: assorted magazines, posterboard, paintbrush, matte medium and brush, and 1 tube of blue acrylic paint
Time: 45 minutes
Size: 10" × 8"

Bleu 4r.

Émission de 1864

INSTRUCTIONS

Grab a bunch of magazines, rifle through them, and tear out bits containing only the colors blue, purple (not mauve), and green (not yellow-green). Make yourself a decent little pile. Stay away from anything figurative–this is about color and form, not about subject.

Working quickly with a brush and matte medium, cover your board with the torn scraps, obliterating the original background. Once that's done, continue to build a collage using only that blue-purple-green range. Consider your placement of the scraps, but don't get too design conscious. It's important to let instincts make the decisions.

Because this piece is an abstraction, you can concentrate totally on mood and composition without worrying about narrative. From time to time, use a little blue paint to get rid of any white tear lines. Keep building layers of torn paper until the time is up. You'll probably be surprised at the outcome when you stand back.

HINT

Because you are only using a limited and harmonious part of the color spectrum, this may appear to be a low-risk piece, but really it's an important task in terms of developing a sense of subtlety. It's easy to get fixated on dramatic creations, but elegant solutions to small problems can often be remarkably satisfying.

When you've finished your "blue" collage, try adding a small amount of orange or vermilion–that will really set the blues tingling.

Expanding the Jabberwocky

'Twas brillig, and the slithy toves...

When Lewis Carroll wrote "Jabberwocky," he created far more than a nonsense poem. He released into our consciousness a stream of characters from an alternative world. It reminds me of one of those toys that you put in water and watch expand. There isn't really that much story there, but by use of gobbledygook and inference, he invites readers to "fill in" their own infinitely expanding interpretation. I once did a pop-up book based on the poem, and all the time I was working on the mechanics and drawings I found myself developing the characters and plot in my head. There was no room to use this expanded version in the six-page book, but the stage and players stayed with me. It started like this:

The Jabberwocky hung from the twisted branch of a Sollomund tree, eggbound and suspended by a single hessian thread that corkscrewed clock- and anti-wise at the wind's whim. For twenty years it pounded its callused snout against the shell's undenting wall, increasingly desperate to break out into the luminous. Yet when it finally cracked open its cage, the creature found itself in utter darkness. For it was deep winter's midnight in the Forest of Thorns and shadow had eaten every scrap of light. The Jabberwocky fell to the forest floor with a cruel thud. Sitting up and casting around its bloodshot eyes, it let out a cry so thick with disappointment that had there been any Pittys within hearing, they would have started a wailing that would have lasted for months.

This heartless entry into the world plunged the Jabberwocky into a profoundly uglyficous mood, a mood that the peoples of Brakenash would rue for half an eternity.

Character by character it grew, and new nonsense words emerged, each needing its own definition and each offering another branch to the tale.

Materials: pen and notebook
Time: 30 to 45 minutes

INSTRUCTIONS

If you don't already know the "Jabberwocky" poem, then give it a read. (It's easy to find online.)

Here are five characters from the poem:

- ▸ the Tumtum tree
- ▸ a slithy tove
- ▸ a Jubjub bird
- ▸ a Bandersnatch
- ▸ a mome rath

Your job is to write a paragraph for each character, describing its appearance and behavior.

HINT

The trick is to let your imagination run. Write whatever comes into your head, just letting the nonsense flow.

Climbing the Steps

Below is a short passage of dialogue. When you've read it, ask the following three questions:

What do these two characters look like?
Who are they?
Where are they going and why?

Even though you have very little information, your imagination will almost certainly kick in, and you'll have begun to develop answers to the three questions even before you've finished reading the passage.

"What happened to level 262?" Robson's high-pitched wheeze punctuated every second word.

"What do you mean what happened to it?" Nonplussed, Dover looked back at his emaciated companion.

"Where did it go?"

"It didn't go anywhere. It's between 261 and 263."

"I know that. I just don't remember anything about it. What was it like?"

"Different."

"Of course it was different. They're all different. Even the ones that start out looking alike end up different. Describe what it looked like."

"I can't."

"Why?"

"I was asleep."

"Asleep! Asleep! But it was your turn to stay awake."

"I know, but I fell asleep anyway. Do you want to go back?"

"Don't start that again."

"What do you mean?"

"You know perfectly well we can't go back—there is no down."

"Well, if there's an up, there must be a down. Stands to logic."

"Have you ever seen the down?"

"No, but that doesn't mean there isn't one."

"Wait a sec. Were you asleep through level 261 as well?"

"No!"

"Well, then, what did the question sign say?"

"Dunno."

"What do you mean? Have you forgotten how to read?"

Materials: pen and notebook, plus whatever you choose to create your visual description

Time: as little as 15 minutes or as long as you care to take

Size: any

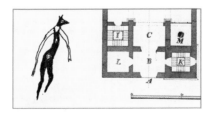

INSTRUCTIONS

Visually express your thoughts about these two characters' appearances. Draw, paint, collage, or even make a model.

Write a paragraph explaining who they are and how they got to the steps.

Write another paragraph describing where they are going and why.

HINT

When engaging in the creative process, try not to get hung up on "How did I do?" "Do I get good marks?" or whatever you do to stop yourself from letting an idea run and simply seeing where your imagination goes. At first, your only job is to record the results.

Later, you'll need to edit–but not until you've got plenty down on paper to work with.

 Big Pastel

The Trickster isn't always going to come to your aid—sometimes you have to trick yourself out of a rut.

Toward the end of my twenties, my art had become so strangled that I was holding my breath for hours at a time. I'd been working mostly in oils, using a very small brush on highly figurative paintings. By the end of each day, I was just about ready to explode. I knew I had to break out from my numbing discipline, but somehow I couldn't seem to do it.

Finally I lost patience with my controlling self and pinned a long sheet of paper to my bedroom wall. I grabbed an old box of chalk pastels that I hadn't touched in years and, without pausing for thought, took a pastel stick in each hand and started attacking the paper with impulsive marks. At first I didn't take much notice of the colors I was selecting or where on the paper I made the marks. I just flailed away, relieved to be doing something physical. I kept going and going, even though my arms were aching like crazy. I didn't think of it as art, just release. But when I finally stepped back a couple of hours later, I was stunned to see that what I'd done was not only very alive, but also not bad at all.

Materials: 5-foot-long paper roll, or 3 large sheets of paper taped together, and box of chalk pastels (medium to hard; soft pastels will break up in your hand)
Time: 1 to 2 hours
Size: approximately 60" x 16"

INSTRUCTIONS

Attach your paper to a wall. (Note to self: not a good idea to do this on the living room wall, as it will leave marks!)

As I described, pick up a pastel stick in each hand and go for it. Have fun, draw lines upon lines, keep alternating left hand, then right hand, then both at once. Pastels are such delicious pure color; fill the white spaces with hues bright and dark. Keep your hands moving. Every now and then put down the pastel sticks and spread the colors into the paper with your fingers. Then return to the pastel wielding. Don't be tempted to step back until your arms have fallen exhausted by your sides.

Enjoy what has passed through you onto the paper.

HINT

Tempting as it might be to start drawing figurative elements, I suggest you keep this particular exercise abstract.

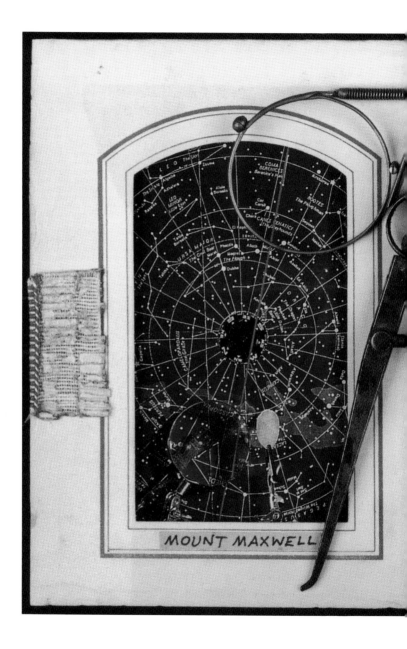

MOUNT MAXWELL

BY STARLIGHT

 Reverse Time Capsules

Embedded in every piece of art is the life lived by the artist during it's creation.

During my mid-twenties, I was working for a month on *Frankie and Johnny*, an oil painting of a banana shooting an apple... I promise there was method and moral in my madness!

Like a fossilized dragonfly caught in amber, the brushstrokes of the painting captured all of my thoughts and all of the events of those four weeks. Even now, looking into the painting's depths, I can recall in detail a BBC radio play about the French resistance, the sounds of an Irish-Swedish couple alternately arguing and making love in the room above, the memory of my cat Ash trying to chew the end of my brush while I retouched the apple's skin, the smell of cinnamon from the kitchen, and the decision I was trying to make about whether to leave one girlfriend in the hope of seducing another.

If our art traps memories, the question arises, "Can the process be reversed?" Can you seed your art in a way that will increase its chances of having personal meaning?

Only one way to find out: **Experiment**

Materials: the usual collage stuff
Time: 1 hour or so
Size: whatever feels comfortable

INSTRUCTIONS

Gather your paint and collage materials to start on a new piece.
Don't premeditate the piece you are about to start.

Put on some music that really gets to you—could be old or new.
Me, I'd probably pick something like "I Heard It Through the Grapevine"
by Marvin Gaye or Leonard Cohen's "Who by Fire."

Next choose something that you know stimulates your sense of
smell, something easy to conjure up—like ground coffee, suntan lotion,
or incense.

Think what else you can do to load the experience.

Once you have set the stage, start to work on your collage.

Let the content and the feel of the work be driven by the music
and the smells.

HINT

Experiment, experiment, experiment. You can adapt this exercise in
any number of ways. Take your headphones and music or audiobook
to the park with a sketchbook. Go to Paris, sit in a café, and
write from your stream of consciousness while you watch people go by.
Climb a tree and use a medicine dropper to splatter inks onto
a canvas below while listening to Puccini.

Above all, make sure you feed your art so that it will feed you.

Childmind

Original thinkers walk a tightrope. Artists, writers, musicians, and inventors are desperately needed, and at the same time, their unconventional thinking can be seen as a threat to the status quo.

If society deems the fruits of imagination worthwhile or pertinent, then it rewards its creator. If it is thought to be irrelevant or, worse, a danger to order, then its inventor is likely to be ignored, ostracized, or—if it's a really bad day—burnt at the stake.

Why else would we teach our children to be so ambivalent toward their creative urges?

So, we learn to shut down, block off our creative dreams and intuitive outpourings, and settle instead for anything that will afford us a stroke from friends and family or a cash reward from the marketplace. But those scraps of reward are a pale relative to the freedoms found in the magnificent/scary landscapes that are revealed when we spread the periphery of our perceptions and wander into the furthest reaches of our imaginations.

To get back our enthusiasm, we first need to remind ourselves of the devil-may-care attitude of our childmind. When young children draw and paint, they do so without artifice and are quite comfortable painting seas purple and people blue—they do not question if their inner landscape is as important as the outer.

To access our childmind is not the same as being childish. Our childmind is the part of us that still knows the value of metaphor and story. In order to listen to our childmind, we first need to quiet the two parrots that sit on our shoulders. The red parrot on our left shoulder speaks with our parents' voice and, among other things, whispers in our ear, "It's all well and good this artsy-fartsy stuff, but it won't end well. You need to be doing something nice and sensible."

The green parrot that sits on your right shoulder constantly squawks things like, "You'll never be good enough, you know. Look at what he's doing, it's so much better than any load of old garbage you might come up with."

Close your eyes and pretend you have a large roll of duct tape, cut off a couple of lengths, and wrap them tightly around the parrots' beaks. You don't have to shoo the birds away, just make sure they shut up while you are trying to concentrate on the inside scoop your childmind is giving you about the creatures that swim in the vibrant purple seas.

Materials: board, 3 tubes of acrylic paint (red, green, and black), and 2 paintbrushes (one size 6 or 7, one size 2)
Time: 20 minutes
Size: 18" high

INSTRUCTIONS

Mix three small cups of paint: one bright red, one bright green, and one black.

Think about the parrots. Think how it felt to paint without fear that you didn't know how, or that someone was going to judge the results of what you did. In a very loose way with the medium-sized brush, quickly paint the two parrots—make them at least a foot high. Then with the smaller brush, paint in a few details, including the duct tape around their beaks.

HINT

While you are doing all of this, I suggest you sing aloud or silently, "Ain't nobody's business but my own."

 Lopsided Lighthouse

There's a game we used to play in the car when my kids were young that we called the alphabet game. Someone would pick a subject, like "countries." We'd then take turns to try to come up with a country that began with each letter of the alphabet: Afghanistan, Belgium, Canada, etc. Extra kudos was gained by coming up with a country that was unusual, ancient, or no longer in existence. Apart from helping the journey pass, it helped everyone's general knowledge.

After a while the game developed, and the categories became more open-ended, like "things you might find in a museum." Imagination became the valued currency, and *S* for "sleeping security (guard)" would get extra credit for alliteration. Alliteration opened further doors of verbal dexterity, and the sound of the words became as important as the subjects.

Materials: **pen and notebook**
Time: **40 minutes (plus)**

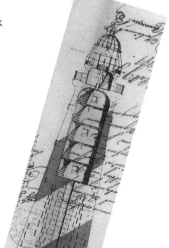

INSTRUCTIONS

Part 1:

Under the category of "things you might find in, on, or next to the sea," start with the letter A and work your way down the alphabet. Write them down as you go.

Make up things like L for "lopsided lighthouse" or X for "'xtra oar in case your rowboat loses one"; let yourself be as inventive as your mood takes you for about 30 minutes.

Part 2:

From the list you've just created, choose five letters that suggest a strong visual image. Then, doodle-sketch five quick little pictures for about 10 minutes. Don't worry about style; just let them be quirky. And if you enjoy the results, it's up to you if you want to illustrate more of the letters.

HINT

If you can get to the point where the words and images start to come at more or less the same time, you've succeeded in getting the two sides of your brain to share information. And that's a big step on the path toward creative dexterity.

 Painting Without Brushes

An old teacher of mine was fond of saying, "The brain is an excellent tool for making sure you get on the right bus, but don't use it for life decisions." He wasn't advocating a total shutdown of the mind, rather a temporary reining in of that part of our brain that's inclined to overrule our intuition, even though our adaptive unconscious would be more suited to dealing with a problem.

One way to convince your brain that it doesn't have all the answers is to give it a task that it finds impossible to gain full mastery over. Take away the tools it knows, and hand it something it hasn't got a clue how to control.

A good brush is an elegant creature, and once you know how to work with it, it can become a vehicle of great precision. But it can also be a tyrant. It may be the prime means of applying paint, but it certainly isn't the only one—almost anything can be used to put paint onto a ground.

I'm going to give you a list of things to paint with that will reduce your control and encourage you to use a more physical/intuitive approach to application. You'll be using paint colors without mixing them, so select your palette with compatibility in mind rather than simply choosing colors you like in isolation.

Materials: posterboard, 7 tubes of acrylic paint (not black or white), paper towel, and the following paint tools: stick from outside, short length of hairy string, your fingers (if this is a problem for you, wear surgical gloves), small spoon, dry ends cut off fruit and vegetables, feather (pigeon would be good), small scrunched-up piece of stiff paper, and short length of wire

Time: 45 minutes

Size: 16" x 12"

INSTRUCTIONS

With a cloth that's been dipped in a thin solution of yellowy-brown acrylic paint, prime the surface of the board to get rid of the flat white background, then tape it to a stiff backing.

Work directly with paint from the tube. Squeeze it out as needed onto the paper towel so that any excess moisture in the paint is absorbed.

Using only the tubes selected, start applying the paint with the various tools. Work at a reasonably quick pace; if the paint isn't drying fast enough, you can always use a hair dryer to speed it up. Imagine you are playing a game of Ping-Pong, always responding to what just happened rather than trying to follow some predetermined plan. When the 45 minutes is up, stop abruptly.

It's quite possible the outcome will seem pretty messy. That doesn't matter – the lesson was designed to grow your reactive skills, not to make a *nice* picture.

HINT

Notice I haven't included a palette knife. That's Van Gogh's fault. His mastery of the knife has led way too many people into believing that if they butter a load of blue and yellow paint on their canvas, they'll automatically end up with a riveting wheat-field landscape.

 Risk and Happy Accidents

For me, knowing what something is going to look like before it's done takes away the potential fun and most of the learning. If I'm working on a collage and I glue down a piece of ephemera that I've been keeping for years and 10 minutes later I cover it with paint, I'm okay with that because I know that it's been buried for a better cause.

If I were able to say, "I don't like that; I'll take it back so that it looks exactly the same way it did," then I would be functioning without real risk. I would have no incentive to plow forward, putting down more and more layers until I ended up in new territory.

Imagine if being able to go back at will was applied to life? We'd never progress past our first vaguely pleasant experience. In fact, we'd probably stay in the womb!

The willingness to take risks sharpens our senses, makes us more liable to commit fully to the work. Risk also leads to "happy accidents": marks and passages that occur only when the work is on the edge of being out of control.

If you want to see simple artistic risk in action, try the following.

Materials: old map or document, old photo of something oddball, and official-looking rubber stamp
Time: an hour or so
Size: 8.5" × 11"

INSTRUCTIONS

Cut your bit of ephemera to the exact size of letter paper. Head down to wherever the nearest color photocopier resides. If you can work the machine yourself, that's good; otherwise, assure the attendant that this won't jam the machine, which means you will need to make sure the edges of your 8.5" x 11" paper are flat and without nicks.

Place the photo facedown on the copier glass and then feed your paper through.

The result will be a map or document with your photo image printed directly onto it. The combined pictorial elements are just too complex to predict, so there will be unexpected relationships and accidents occurring all over the page.

Once you have your dubious document, you may want to work into it further with inks, paint, or pencil before you add a rubber stamping. The results are often bizarre creations that satisfyingly defy origin and purpose.

HINT

I'll sometimes go further and coat my abominations with melted beeswax and old yellowed varnish. It enriches the color, protects the surface, and makes it smell good too!

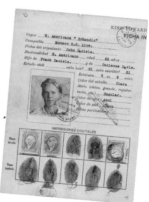

 Delivered by Accident in Twilight

When Michelangelo was asked to describe his sculpting method, he answered, "I am merely releasing the figures from the stone."

His rival, Leonardo, had a much more analytical overview of nature, yet he too was known to derive his inspiration from his materials. There is a story told about the newly applied plaster for a fresco the master was about to work on. As the plaster began to dry, an unsightly stain started to emerge. The plasterer apologized and said that he would scrape it clean and replace it. Leonardo wouldn't let him touch it; instead, he sat on a stool in front of the stain and contemplated it for three days. At last he arose and began the painting using the shape of the stain as the basis for his composition.

At school most of us were taught to develop an image in our heads and then try to replicate it on paper. That's an incredibly difficult task, one that puts many people off art for life—and, if the two greats of the Renaissance are anything to go by, not necessarily the only approach to making things.

The most powerful art often comes from dropping predetermined ideas of what something will look like. When people stop seeing themselves in the role of conceiver and switch to the notion that they are the conduit through which the work will pass, the pressure of responsibility is released. Once this happens, it's amazing how the things we make can surprise and inform us.

Materials: variety of nature magazines, glue stick, wooden board, cheesecloth or muslin, staple gun, acrylic paints (and possibly chalk pastel), paper towel, and matte medium and brush
Time: a couple of hours to start, but be prepared for it to be ongoing
Size: 24" x 16"

INSTRUCTIONS

From the magazines, tear out a bunch of images of natural elements with rich colors. Rip them up and paste them onto your board fairly randomly until you have it covered. Don't be too concerned about the collage's appearance because it will soon be semi-screened under a shroud. If there are bubbles in the paper when it dries, pierce them with a blade and work the air out with your thumb. Once the surface is flat, stretch taut a piece of cheesecloth or muslin over the front of your picture and staple it to the back of the board with a staple gun. When it's secure and tight, your picture will be only partially visible through the creamy mesh. Now cover it in a couple coats of matte medium. This will hold it firm and give you a finely abraded ground to work on.

Prop the picture up against a wall so that you can see it from a few feet away. Look at it long and hard. You have your equivalent of Leonardo's fresco stain. What can you see? Stare at it till your mind blanks and you are no longer thinking about what you are meant to be doing. If you are patient, you will eventually start to see shapes within the shapes. Start emphasizing those shapes by painting into them.

Squeeze paint out as needed onto the paper towel so that any excess moisture is absorbed. Use your paint fairly dry and drag it across the picture's gauzy surface. The paint will catch but only in places (this is called "scumbling"). Try to magnify edges within the subtle terrain, working the faint outlines up until they become solid; keep going until the picture's personality emerges. Don't prejudge it; don't edit it with your own agenda–just help the forms and images come gradually forward.

This is not an exercise to be hurried. The amount of time you spend looking at your picture should be far greater than the amount you spend painting. If you struggle with the dry paint, try chalk pastel, which also works well on stretched, matted cheesecloth.

This painting may take a few hours or a few days or even longer– be patient. I've had paintings take years before they fully emerge.

HINT

I realize this might seem somewhat esoteric and even a little New Age, but if it worked back in the fifteenth century for two undoubted geniuses, the mechanics can't be that flaky.

Seduction Optional

In 1933, Jun'ichirō Tanizaki wrote these words in an essay comparing aesthetics in Japan and the West:

> Yet for better or for worse we do love things that bear the marks of grime, soot, and weather, and we love the colors and the sheen that call to mind the past that made them.

Tanizaki came from a time and place where there was a deep appreciation for patina and the way architecture and objects often become more beautiful with age and touch, their surfaces becoming worn-round or oiled-smooth, making them soft to the eye. He pointed out how different that Japanese longing for gentle muteness was to the Western preference for a harsh-lit, shiny, and hard-edged aesthetic.

In Italian art, the term *sfumato* means "smoky." It's used to describe the area of transition between a shadow and the light it enters—where clear edge is impossible to locate and the eye is forced to soften its focus.

Patina and sfumato are all around us, but we move so quickly we all but block it out. We are missing so much.

Materials: none that you might carry
Time: yes
Size: everywhere

INSTRUCTIONS

Now that this "softness" has been brought to your more immediate
attention, take your time and go hunting for patina and sfumato.
When you find patina, touch it. It's as good to the fingers as to the
eyes. And when you spy sfumato, lose yourself in its borderlands,
where one thing touches another.

HINT

A sensualist is a person who lingers on, and in, the brink.

L O C K S.

Fig. 6.

Fig.

Fig. 5.

AND THEN...

If you finished all 49 exercises, you will have undoubtedly traveled far and hopefully learned much from the Trickster and his irascible methodology. Take a bow, savor the applause, but please don't stop there–your journey has only just begun.

Whatever you wish to create, create it. Set your dreams way beyond your expectations.

If you follow your soul's path, there will be many rewards, though they will rarely be what you expect.

Even if you give your best, there will be times when intelligence, knowledge, and a sense of hope feel as if they have been sucked out of you. It's not always easy to keep going when faced with indifference or to watch values being defined by a mass infatuation with mediocrity. But it's not your job to define taste. Don't be disheartened: what matters is the integrity with which you pursue your art (whatever form that takes).

Step back, stay composed, breathe, and watch the larger rhythms– don't push against the river; go with its flow, and let it carry you to sea. The Trickster may be contrary, but he never fights the current.

You will have breakthrough moments when you intuitively understand the new, when you find a way to remove a limitation you've placed on yourself, and when you realize that a lifetime's worth of baggage can simply be set down... allowing you to walk on unencumbered.

Enjoy the journey, take pleasure in your companions, and always remember to look in your hat.

INDEX OF THE FAMILIARS

Am   Arbah   Atafo   Babylon   Chog   The Corks

Coy   Dante   Dennis   Dikle   Easter   Elmer

Fiji   Flash'arry   Fork   The 4 Fazes   Fritz   Gilbert

The Gok Twins   Halt   Hitchcock   Hook   Hopit   Katie

Keybone   Leaferikson   Lux   Maluku   Manith   Marshall

Maug   Monty   Motu On   Pee-Jay   Pelicos   Perez

The Point   Poka   Punt   Quepol   Samoa   Sharp

Sliver   Stickler   Stretch   Talismon   Threepence   Tinker   Tox

Treen   Vini, Vidi & Vici   Wallis & Tuna   Wip   The Wormers   Yap

Nick Bantock is the author of twenty-five books, eleven of which have appeared on the bestseller lists. *Griffin & Sabine* stayed on the bestseller list for over two years. His works have been translated into thirteen languages and more than five million copies have been sold throughout the world.

Once named by the classic sci-fi magazine *Weird Tales* as one of the best storytellers of the century, Nick has had paintings, drawings, sculptures, collages and prints exhibited in shows in the United Kingdom, France, and North America, and his works hang in numerous private collections.

Nick has also worked in a betting shop in the East End of London, trained as a psychotherapist, and designed and had built a house that combined an Indonesian temple and a Russian orthodox church with an English cricket pavilion and a New Orleans bordello. Between 2007 and 2010, he was one of the twelve committee members responsible for selecting Canada's postage stamps.

Among other things, he can't swim, he's never ridden a horse, his spelling is dreadful, and his singing voice is as flat as a pancake.